The Private Company Today

An investigation into the economic position of the unquoted company in the United Kingdom

A J Merrett and M E Lehr

DIRECTORS BOOKSHELF

First published in Britain by Gower Press Limited
140 Great Portland Street, London W1N 5TA
1971

ISBN 0 7161 0039 8

Set in 11 on 13 Bembo and Printed in Britain by A. Wheaton & Company, Exeter

Contents

Figures

Introduction

This book is concerned with the present role and future survival of the private company in the UK. The situation it reveals can be summarised into two central statements of fact:

1 The private companies and businesses make a large and special contribution to the UK economy
2 The current trend of tax legislation, if continued unchanged, will ultimately eliminate all private businesses of any significant size

Having established these facts, the book outlines a new tax policy which will keep in balance the need both to tax wealth and to protect the sources of that wealth. The argument is no more than a restatement of Aesop's fable: don't kill the goose that lays the golden eggs.

The research that underlies this book arose from a commission by a group of directors of leading private companies (the Unquoted Companies Group) for the authors to estimate the size and assess the economic role and future of the private company in the UK economy. The primary role of the study was simply to assess statistically and in economic terms the contribution of the UK-controlled unquoted sector of the economy, and in particular the private company, to employment, profits and the efficient operation of the UK economy. The results of the research form Part 1 of this book. Nationally available statistics are not specifically designed to reveal information on this sector of the economy and much of the analysis has involved using very rudimentary tools to estimate breakdowns and obtain additional information. It is hoped that the more detailed statistical analyses of the Bolton Committee and subsequent research will provide substantially more detail to enable refinement of the analysis presented here.

Part 2 is concerned with the ultimate effects of present and possible future fiscal legislation upon the private company, as it is principally on such legislation that the future of these companies turns. Whilst this is a highly emotive subject, an attempt has been made to confine these chapters to questions of numerical fact concerning the impact of present legislation and an estimation of costs and benefits that would arise from a continuation of this trend or from a proposed change in taxation policy.

This book does, not, however, concern itself with what many would regard as the central political issue, namely the importance of the private company in terms of the opportunities that it offers to successive generations of talented people and as a factor in the preservation of personal liberty.

A J Merrett
M E Lehr
December 1970

Part One

Role of the Private Company

Chapter One
Summary of Research Findings

The first half of this book reports the findings of original research into the economic contribution of the private company and business (for convenience, where the inclusiveness, is obvious, we shall refer to all such enterprises as private companies). For ease of reference, the main findings are summarised below. It must, however, be emphasised that some of these conclusions are subject to qualifications which are fully described in the following three chapters.

Numbers

1 The overwhelming majority of registered companies are small private companies. Less than 2 per cent of all companies are public quoted companies. Less than 1.5 per cent of all companies are "large" private companies—using the Board of Trade definition of "large" as those with net assets exceeding £0.5M or annual income greater than £50 000

Employment

2 More people work for private companies and businesses than for any other type of employer. Private companies and businesses account for 39 per cent of civil employment, as compared with public companies' 37 per cent, nationalised industries' 10 per cent, the civil service's 11 per cent and overseas companies' 3 per cent

3 Private companies and businesses are the predominant employers, in the service industries, but a smaller employer than the public company in manufacturing. Of the total employed in the private sector, private companies and businesses account for 71 per cent of those in industries such as financial services,

hotels and catering; 54 per cent of those in retailing and wholesaling; and 38 per cent of those in manufacturing and allied industries

Profitability

4 Private companies and businesses contribute 40 per cent of the total profits generated by all enterprises, while private companies alone account for 83 per cent, 64 per cent and 51 per cent of all company profits in the transport and communication, construction and distributive industries respectively

5 While encompassing large numbers of small enterprises, the unquoted sector also includes over 2000 "large" companies which account for 5 per cent of civil employment and 10 per cent of total corporate profits

Efficiency

6 The "large" private company is more efficient than the public company. The large private company has higher rates of return on total assets in eleven out of fifteen industry groups (73 per cent). The efficiency of the private company is most marked in metal manufacture, food and drink, where the returns are 77 per cent, 44 per cent and 43 per cent higher respectively than those of public companies

Special contributions

7 Private companies are essential to the maintenance of free competition in the economy. Their numbers, diversity and limited share ownership are substantial barriers to the progress of potential monopolies

8 Private companies are more important innovators in products, marketing and production than their size would indicate. The common identity of management and ownership in such organisations creates a motivational drive and willingness to take risks, which are the characteristic requirements for innovation

9 In small fragmented markets, the private company is a more efficient unit of activity than the larger public company. For this reason, private companies take a leading part in the development of such industries as construction, engineering or financial and professional services

Chapter Two

The Private Sector of Industry

In this study "private companies and businesses" comprise companies whose shares are not quoted on stock exchanges, together with the range of enterprises (partnerships and sole traders) operating without the benefit of company status. To assess the importance of this sector of the economy, this chapter analyses the available statistics on the numbers of private companies, the amount of employment created by private companies and businesses, and their contribution to the total profits of British industry.

Numbers of private companies

Although the total number of limited companies is an annually published figure, there has been no detailed analysis of its make-up since 1961. Since then the total of registered companies has risen by over 30 per cent, and to that extent the available statistics are out of date. Nevertheless they still give a broadly accurate indication of the characteristics of the situation that exists today.

The total number of registered companies in Great Britain at the end of 1961 was around 397 000, as shown in Figure 2:1. This includes all companies registered in the UK other than those without share capital (mainly charitable institutions and clubs which are of no economic relevance). In this total, however, each subsidiary is counted as a separate company. When the companies are consolidated so that the parent and its subsidiaries are counted as one, the number of companies (financial units) is reduced to 296 400.

Less than 2 per cent of the companies or financial units are accounted for by public quoted companies, while 275 000 out of the 296 400 total are what were classified in 1961 as private exempt companies—that is, those that have less than fifty shareholders and which prohibit any invitation to the

	Number of companies	Number of financial units[1]
Quoted: public companies	5 100	4 800
Unquoted: public companies	5 600	4 200
private non-exempt companies	41 500	12 400
private exempt companies	345 000	275 000
TOTAL	397 200[2]	296 400

FIGURE 2:1 NUMBER OF UK COMPANIES, 1961

[1] Financial units count the parent and its subsidiaries as one company
[2] The total excludes some 5100 companies without share capital (mainly charitable institutions and trusts of no economic importance)
Source: "Patterns of Company Finance," *Economic Trends*, November 1967

public to become shareholders. (The exemption referred to the right—abolished by the 1967 Companies Act—for a company not to file accounts if it conformed to certain qualifications.)

Employment by private companies and businesses

From an economic point of view, the most generally useful measure of the relative sizes of private (unquoted) and public (quoted) sectors is the contribution each makes to the total employment of the UK economy. Given the wide variation in capital intensity between different economic activities (all of them essential in a developed economy), figures such as total capital employed by sector would convey a misleading impression. Full employment, however, is a major objective of economic policy, so that, assuming that the balance of activities in the economy is in some sense optimal, the proportions of employment accounted for by different sectors are meaningful and significant figures.

Information is sometimes quoted on the employment accounted for by "small" firms (as for example, in the CBI pamphlet *Britain's Small Firms—Their Vital Role in the Economy*), but this is misleading for a number of reasons. First, the definition of small is purely arbitrary (typically less than 200 employees). Second, and more important, however, is that the coverage of such statistics is limited—the information relates only to individuals employed in the so-called census industries, which account for little more than half of total employment in the UK. They wholly exclude those employed in agriculture, transportation, wholesaling, insurance, banking, finance, catering and hotels. Moreover, some 1.6M people, 8 per cent of the labour force in the private sectors, are self-employed and less than half of these are in census of production and distribution figures.

Official figures do not attempt to allocate employment between the unquoted and quoted sectors, and attention thus tends to be directed towards the sector for which detailed figures of profits, assets, etc, are available—namely quoted public industrial companies.

The following tables are based on the amalgamation of employment data from the censuses of production and distribution (for the industries which they cover), Department of Employment statistics, a sample survey of the accounts of the "large" private companies, and estimates based on the accounts of public companies.

Although the figures are inevitably very approximate, there is every reason to believe that the overall picture given in Figure 2:2 provides a substantially accurate indication of the distribution of employment as it stood in 1966. Furthermore, although there has been a drift of employment away from the private unquoted company, the situation has not changed markedly since 1966.

Overseas-owned companies are in a distinct economic category and the estimated employment accounted for them has been shown separately. On technical grounds, of course, they are private companies, but they have little else in common with the independent UK-controlled private company. They are in fact similar to the subsidiaries of UK public companies.

Figure 2:2 shows that the UK-controlled private sector as a whole (quoted and unquoted) accounts for 76 per cent of all the employment in the economy, the balance being made up by nationalised industries (10 per cent), national and local government, teaching, etc (11 per cent), and overseas-controlled companies (3 per cent). Of this 76 per cent, over half (39 per cent), is estimated to be in private companies and businesses, compared with the public quoted companies' 37 per cent. In numbers, the 39 per cent accounted for by the private company is 9.65M people, out of a total labour force of 24.91M.

In spite of the greater scale of production and investment by public companies and the nationalised industries, it is clear that the larger number of private companies and businesses are a major force in providing employment.

No detailed breakdown of employment by quoted and unquoted sectors

	Millions	% of total civil employment
Private (unquoted) companies and businesses	9.65	39
Public (quoted) companies	9.15	37
TOTAL PRIVATE SECTOR	18.80	76
Nationalised industries	2.59	10
National and local government	2.67	11
TOTAL PUBLIC SECTOR	5.26	21
Employed by overseas-controlled companies	0.85	3
TOTAL POPULATION IN CIVIL EMPLOYMENT	24.91	100

FIGURE 2:2 DISTRIBUTION OF TOTAL EMPLOYMENT, 1966
Sources: *Employment and Productivity Gazette,* November 1966; Census of production 1963; Census of distribution 1966; Sample of quoted and unquoted companies

in different industries is possible with the existing information; the best that can be attempted is a very approximate breakdown (shown in Figure 2:3) into industrial, retailing and wholesaling transportation, agricultural and "other" (mainly professional services, insurance, banking etc). These figures suggest that the private companies and businesses account for 38 per cent of private sector industrial employment, 54 per cent of retailing and wholesaling, 58 per cent of transport and communication, and virtually 100 per cent of agriculture.

The breakdown of employment within the private companies and businesses is shown in the third column of the table. There it is seen that 40 per cent of employment by these enterprises is industrial, and that industry, agriculture and transport together account for 51 per cent. While retailing and wholesaling are commonly associated with the private company, it is seen from the table that they account for only 18 per cent of its total employment.

It is not possible to break down employment in the unquoted sector into its

	Private companies and businesses millions	Public companies millions	Private companies & businesses as % total private companies and businesses	Private companies & businesses as % private sector
Industrial	3.90	6.26	40	38
Retailing & wholesaling	1.75	1.47	18	54
Agriculture	0.75	neg	8	100
Transport & communication	0.28	0.20	3	58
Other	2.97	1.22	31	71
TOTAL	9.65	9.15	100	51

FIGURE 2:3 BREAKDOWN OF PRIVATE SECTOR EMPLOYMENT, 1966

corporate and non-corporate parts; information on small private companies is too fragmentary. Nevertheless the analysis of a sample of "large" private company accounts suggested that the employment accounted for by these companies in manufacturing, distribution and transportation was around 0.95M. For Board of Trade purposes, a company is considered "large" if its net assets exceed £0.5M or its annual income is greater than £50 000. The absence of a pre-existing detailed classification of large private companies outside these areas makes an assessment of their contribution to employment extremely difficult. In broad terms, however, it might be estimated at around 0.25M. On this basis the large private companies would account for approximately 1.2M of the 9.65M, employment in the whole unquoted sector, that is approximately 5 per cent of total civil employment.

Profits contributed by private companies and businesses

Assessing the relative importance of quoted and unquoted sectors by profits is a matter of considerable difficulty. Corporate gross profits are determined as a residual after the various costs of production, including management, have been subtracted from income. With sole traders and partnerships this is not so; the residual income accruing to the proprietor represents both profit and an implicit charge for management—there is no distinction between the two. Even with the smaller private company, where a legal distinction is made, reported profits are not comparable with those of quoted companies. The salaries of executive directors, where these have substantial shareholdings in the company, may be determined solely by the incidence of taxation, and may bear only a limited relation to the economic worth of the directors of the company.

Another major problem is that a public company may draw profitability from a range of overseas interests and nevertheless remain a UK company. Overseas profits are economically quite different from profits arising wholly in this country since, with the former, overseas countries and their fiscal authorities are the main beneficiaries in terms of taxes and employment. Since this is not a significant phenomenon among private companies, the reported profits of the two sectors are not directly comparable.

Finally, it should be noted that profits are an inherently ambiguous indicator of size. Consider, for example, a company making a profit of £x on given total sales. The adoption of a more labour-saving method of production at the expense of considerably more capital might save, say, £y in labour costs after additional depreciation is charged. By the standard of profitability it would seem that the company had become bigger, since with no change in sales its reported profits would have risen from £x to £$x + y$. In fact it may have done nothing more than substitute one factor of production (capital) for another (labour), with no economic benefit to the community; reported profits take no account of the cost of the capital employed in the operation. It is in the light of these very considerable qualifications that the statistics on gross trading profits in Figure 2:4 should be viewed.

Total corporate profits arising within the UK are known, but the official figures give no breakdown of these by sector. However, the profits of large public companies operating wholly or mainly in the UK are available, and these will approximate to profits arising in the UK of public companies. The figures will include some overseas income, but will exclude the UK profits of companies mainly operating overseas. Furthermore, the large public companies account for the bulk of profits in the public sector. The size of the large public company sample in 1966 was 2109. For comparison there were only 3157 ordinary and deferred UK-quoted securities, of industrial, commercial, and financial companies in relevant categories (not includ-

	Gross profits arising in UK	Annual depreciation	Net profits
	£m	£m	£m
PUBLIC COMPANIES	3161	695	2466
PRIVATE BUSINESSES			
Private companies	1352	492	860
Non-corporate enterprises	660	299	361
TOTAL PRIVATE COMPANIES & BUSINESSES	2012	791	1221

FIGURE 2:4 BREAKDOWN OF PROFITS BY SECTOR, 1966

Source: National Income and Expenditure, 1968
Statistics on Incomes, Prices, Employment and Production, June 1968

ing for example, overseas mining companies) a significant proportion of which would in any case be operating mainly overseas.

The profits of the non-corporate sector have been estimated by subtracting from income from self-employment (£2562M in 1966), a notional salary of £1200 for each of the 1.58 million in self-employment in 1966. This is slightly above the average salary in manufacturing in that year, and, given the considerable variation of size and profitability in the non-corporate sector, it is probably of the right order of magnitude. On this basis the gross profits of sole traders and partnerships were about £660M. If the notional salary were put at £1500, non-corporate profits would be only £192M. This compared with gross profits of public companies of £3161M and of private companies of £1352M.

The comparison of gross profits in column 1, however, gives a misleading impression and column 3 gives estimated net profits after the deduction of annual depreciation. In terms of net profits, public companies are about twice as large as private businesses.

Private company profits by size

The analysis of profits made by private companies (see Figure 2:5) shows how important is the relatively small category—in terms of numbers—of large private companies. As mentioned earlier, for Board of Trade purposes a company is considered "large" if its net assets exceed £0.5M or its income is greater than £50 000 a year.

In the case of the exempt companies, however, where the information is drawn from an Inland Revenue survey, "large" is defined simply as having profits *assessable to tax* in excess of £50 000. As profits assessable to tax will generally be substantially less than gross income (before depreciation), it is almost certain that there are more than 1024 private exempt companies, shown in Figure 2:5, which would meet the less strict standard of simply having gross profits in excess of £50 000. Moreover, the definition of "large" in the case of the private exempt companies involves no size qualification (like having net assets in excess of £0.5M as in the case of the large non-exempt companies). This too would increase the number of private exempt companies to be counted as "large" on the £50 000 of gross income or £0.5M of net assets definition, employed elsewhere in the table. It is unlikely however that this inconsistency of definition involves any significant alteration of the overall picture presented in Figure 2:5.

On this by no means exacting definition, only 4424 or 1.5 per cent of the 296 400 companies (financial units) would count as "large". Eliminating those owned or controlled by overseas interests the number of large companies is reduced to 4192 or 1.4 per cent of the total. These, however, accounted for 67 per cent of all the trading profits of UK companies operating in the UK in 1962. Of these the UK-owned large public companies are seen to account for 57 per cent of total trading profits and the private 10 per cent.

While there are some discrepancies of definition it is probably that the smaller private companies accounted for a further 20 per cent of the total £3819M of trading profits. On this basis, private companies (excluding foreign controlled companies) accounted for about 30 per cent of total trading profits compared with the public companies' 57 per cent.

Private company profits by industry

As mentioned earlier profits are an ambiguous indicator of size, and it is in the light of the qualifications listed there that the statistics on gross trading profits given in Figure 2:6 should be viewed. Bearing these qualifications in mind it is seen from the table that overall the total profits of the private

	Number of companies	Number of financial units[1]	UK-owned industrial and commercial "large" companies			
			Number	% of total	Gross profits £m 1962	Gross profits as % of UK total
Quoted:						
public companies	5 100	4 800	2 170	51	2189	57%
Unquoted:						
public companies	5 600	4 200				
private non-exempt companies	41 500	12 400	998	24	250	10% (private non-exempt and private exempt companies)
private exempt companies	345 000	275 000	1 024	25	134	
TOTAL	397 200[2]	296 400	4 192	100	2573	67%
Total trading profits of all companies operating in UK					3819	100%

FIGURE 2:5 PROFIT CONTRIBUTION OF UK COMPANIES, 1962

[1] Financial units count the parent and its subsidiaries as one company

[2] The total excludes some 5 100 companies without share capital (mainly charitable institutions and trusts of no economic importance)

Source: "Patterns of Company Finance," *Economic Trends*, November 1967

	By public companies	All companies	Private companies (estimated)	Private companies as % of total
	£m	£m	£m	
Distributive trades	406	836	430	51
Transport and communication	47	273	226	83
Engineering and electrical goods	477	617	140	23
Construction	75	208	133	64
Metal manufacture	186	283	97	34
Food, drink and tobacco	460	511	51	10
Paper, printing and publishing	179	225	46	30
Metal goods not elsewhere spec	136	174	38	12
Vehicles	162	192	30	15
Clothing and footwear	49	66	17	26
Other manufacturing industries	77	93	16	17
Timber, furniture, etc	22	32	10	31
Leather, leather goods and fur	4	12	8	66
Shipbuilding and marine engineer	7	13	6	46
Bricks, pottery, glass, etc	129	132	3	2
Chemicals and allied industries	416	395	neg	neg
Textiles	193	180	neg	neg
Total companies in manufacturing and distribution operating in UK	3025	4242	1217	29
Financial companies, services etc		271		
Total corporate gross trading profits arising in UK		4513		
Rent and non-trading income		1359		
Income from abroad		1401		
Total corporate income		7273		

FIGURE 2:6 GROSS TRADING PROFITS OF COMPANIES BY INDUSTRY GROUP, 1966

companies in the industrial and distributive industries amounted to 29 per cent of total corporate profits in these industries.

The industry by industry figures must, however, be regarded with reserve in some cases. Not only do the public company figures exclude "small" public companies, a comparatively minor source of error, but they are allocated to the industry to which they *principally* belong. The private company figures are derived by subtracting these public companies' profits from the total profits for each industry. (The latter are derived from the Inland Revenue statistics which allocate each *subsidiary* to its appropriate industry category).

These figures do, however, serve to indicate the industrial areas in which the private company is particularly important in terms of profits; these are distribution, transportation and construction, in which it accounts for over half of total profits of all companies. These three industries are similarly important in terms of total profits, accounting for £430M, £226M and £133M respectively. Engineering at £140M is also substantial.

"Top ten" private companies

The analysis in this chapter has given some idea in statistical terms of size and economic importance of the private company. In particular they highlight the large contribution made to the community by large private companies. Although they only represent 1.4 per cent of all companies, they account for 5 per cent of civil employment and 10 per cent of profits.

To identify some of the main companies which fall within this group, tables have been compiled and are reproduced in the Appendix which list the "Top Ten" (or fewer) companies within each industry with total assets of more than £500 000. It is not claimed that the list is exhaustive, particularly as regards previously "exempt" companies. Nevertheless the tables do give a generally accurate indication of the major private UK-owned companies. They are seen to include companies of national—in some cases international—reputation in almost every industry, from advanced electronics (Ferranti) through construction (McAlpine and Wates), to glass (Pilkington), materials handling (Lansing Bagnall), mail order (Littlewoods), newspapers (*Daily Telegraph*) and retailing (Sainsburys). (The list relates to 1967 and since that date Pilkingtons have been obliged to seek a quotation.)

Chapter Three

A Comparison of Private Companies with Public Companies

The efficiency of companies must be judged ultimately by the overall efficiency with which they use the financial resources at their disposal. Measures of efficiency such as rate of growth of sales or technological achievement are inconclusive in themselves because their value must ultimately be measured in economic terms. It could be the case that the cost of the achievement in terms of economic resources utilised outweighs the economic benefit.

For capital-intensive companies (and this covers most of the companies classified in the previous chapter as "large") economic efficiency can best be judged in terms of return on capital. The logic of this is that return on capital represents profit as a percentage of capital, and capital is basically both what is at risk and the only "unpaid for" factor of production, in that no interest charge has been deducted from profit at this stage.

Measuring efficiency

The most revealing measure of operating efficiency is to take profits, pre-tax and interest, but net of depreciation, as a percentage of total assets—that is to say, the items of property, plant, machinery, stock and debtors which constitute the right-hand side of the balance sheet. This ratio, therefore, effectively measures profits (before interest and taxation) relative to total assets employed, irrespective of the method by which these are financed or of the taxes borne. For example, the ratio would be the same whether the company were primarily financed by ordinary share capital or by bank borrowing, or whether it had a high or low average tax rate.

This ratio can be contrasted with the overall measure of efficiency represented by the net of tax profits to equity employed. The latter is simply that part of the capital of the company subscribed by shareholders or retained from profits. In effect this ratio measures not only operating but also financing efficiency, because it depends on how much the company has relied upon debt capital and minimal tax charges rather than upon making demands on equity shareholders.

In the following analysis of the efficiency of public and private companies the accent is on the return on total assets so that in effect only operating efficiency is being measured. The reason for this is that it is extremely difficult to get significant comparisons of overall efficiency—that is, taking into account differences in financing efficiency as between public and private companies. The net of tax return on equity capital would not reflect differences in financing efficiency as between public and private companies (as it would between public companies) because tax legislation frequently dictates entirely different tax strategies for the two types of company.

Social welfare aspect

While keeping taxation to a minimum and utilising the cheapest forms of finance are evidently important to shareholders, the most critical aspect of efficiency from the standpoint of *social welfare* is that of operating efficiency as measured by return on total assets. This is simply because the community as a whole gains no advantage from a company's reducing its tax burden or by its securing a larger share of the nation's limited supply of loan finance; these are methods by which the company secures the maximum slice of the cake for its own shareholders. From the standpoint of the community it is evidently the size of the cake which matters, which is unaltered by the method of financing or by tax minimisation. This, however, is in no way to deprecate the value of loan finance to private companies and the extent to which the latter have utilised such finance to make important contributions to the economy. The following analysis is, therefore, primarily in terms of return on total assets.

Anomalies in the data

The data—drawn from the reports and accounts of companies—is inevitably subject to the limitations of its sources. For example, the fixed assets in the balance sheets will have been purchased over a number of years, and since they are recorded in the balance sheet at their original cost and costs have been rising continuously over the last thirty years, their book value may differ as between one company and another for no other reason than that their assets were purchased at different dates. Correction of the balance sheet data to bring all the assets up to their current market value would not, however, very substantially affect the total values of fixed assets as between one company and another. All companies are affected to some degree, and it is only when the age structure of the fixed assets of a firm diverges greatly from its industry's norm that anomalous results will occur. Also the overall effect as regards any individual company is less than proportionate to the revision of the fixed assets figures, since around half of the total assets will be stocks and debtors—and neither of these is subject to correction.

A more significant source of distortion can arise from differences in depreciation policy and stock valuation. Accepted accounting practice permits significant variations in the rates at which companies depreciate their assets and in the method by which they value their stocks. Over-depreciation of assets and under-valuation of stocks can very substantially reduce reported profitability. Moreover, the fragmentary evidence available suggests that over-depreciation and under-valuation are far more common in private than public companies, because the former are not under the same shareholder pressure as the latter to maintain a high level of reported profitability. They have instead considerable incentives from the close-company legislation referred to above and also from the desire to minimize corporation tax liability to state their profits conservatively. Such conservatism on the part of private companies, however, tends to reinforce rather than contradict the conclusions which follow and no attempt is made to correct it.

Sample of public and private companies

The basis of the assessment of relative efficiency is the sample of companies used by the Board of Trade for the data given in the publication *Statistics on Incomes, Prices, Employment and Production.* A complete analysis would require detailed financial data for both exempt and non-exempt parts of the private company sector. However those companies that were previously exempt had only begun filing accounts in 1969 and a detailed analysis was not practicable. Furthermore the Board of Trade specifically excludes from this analysis companies involved in agriculture, mining and quarrying, property, insurance, banking and finance, and those operating wholly or mainly overseas.

Both public and private non-exempt samples were intended to be exhaustive samples of companies with either assets of £0.5M or more, or gross income of £50 000 or more. As there are so many private companies, it is extremely difficult to keep the samples up to date and borderline companies have escaped the net, particularly in the larger private sector. Nevertheless it is thought that the private company sample in 1966 comprised about 80 per cent of those falling in the relevant size range.

The private sample of the Board of Trade is not directly usable since it contains a large number of companies not relevant to our inquiry, including some 404 subsidiaries of overseas companies. As mentioned earlier these exhibit financial and operating characteristics markedly different from UK-owned companies. There are also a number of public unquoted companies which must be removed from the sample before it meets the desired criteria. The remaining 311 companies are all comparatively large UK-owned private companies that did not enjoy exempt status before the 1967 Finance Act.

The breakdown of the sample by the numbers of companies in each industry is shown in Figure 3:1. From this it is seen that the number of large private companies in some categories of industry is very small—for example, there is only one in the leather and fur goods industry and only two in the vehicles industry.

Given that companies may vary substantially in size, the number of each type of company in each industry has, of course, no direct bearing on their relative importance to that industry. In the more highly capital-intensive types of company covered by the sample, the relative importance of each different type of company in each industry is probably best indicated by their total assets and by relating these assets to those of quoted companies. This information is shown in Figures 3:2 and 3:3.

It may be seen from Figure 3:2 that in a number of industries the total assets of the "large" private non-exempt companies are substantial. In four industries—chemicals, bricks, pottery and glass, construction and wholesale distribution—the total assets in this sector exceed £100M. This is not simply a reflection of the larger size of these industries, for when the private sample is compared with the public sample its importance is highlighted further. The relative size of the "large" private sector in each industry is shown in Figure 3:3. From this is seen that relative to the public companies the large private companies are 17 per cent in the construction industry, 13 per cent in bricks, pottery and glass, 9 per cent in wholesale and retail distribution and 7 per cent in transport.

Industry	Large private companies		Large public companies	
	Number of firms	% of sample	Number of firms	% of sample
Food	13	4.2	62	3.0
Drink	11	3.5	76	3.6
Chemicals	26	8.4	90	4.3
Metal manufacture	10	3.2	92	4.4
Non-electrical engineering	31	10.0	249	11.9
Electrical engineering	11	3.5	107	5.1
Shipbuilding and marine engineering	4	1.3	25	1.2
Vehicles	2	0.6	56	2.7
Other metal goods	15	4.8	125	5.9
Textiles	22	7.1	188	8.9
Leather and fur goods	1	0.3	17	0.8
Clothing and footwear	6	1.9	78	3.7
Bricks, pottery and glass	7	2.3	92	4.4
Timber	10	3.2	65	3.1
Paper, printing and publishing	27	8.7	105	5.0
Other manufacturing	9	2.9	73	3.5
Construction	22	7.1	106	5.0
Transport	14	4.5	36	1.7
Wholesale distribution	34	10.9	190	9.0
Retail distribution	21	6.8	149	7.1
Miscellaneous services	15	4.8	120	5.7
TOTAL IN SAMPLE	311	100.0	2101	100.0

FIGURE 3:1 BREAKDOWN OF SAMPLES

Comparative rates of return

In order to assess their relative efficiency by reference to rates of return earned by different types of company, it is first necessary to exclude from the comparison, as far as possible, extraneous factors which may contribute to differences of rate of return. Here the major factor comes probably from differences in the industrial composition of the companies being compared

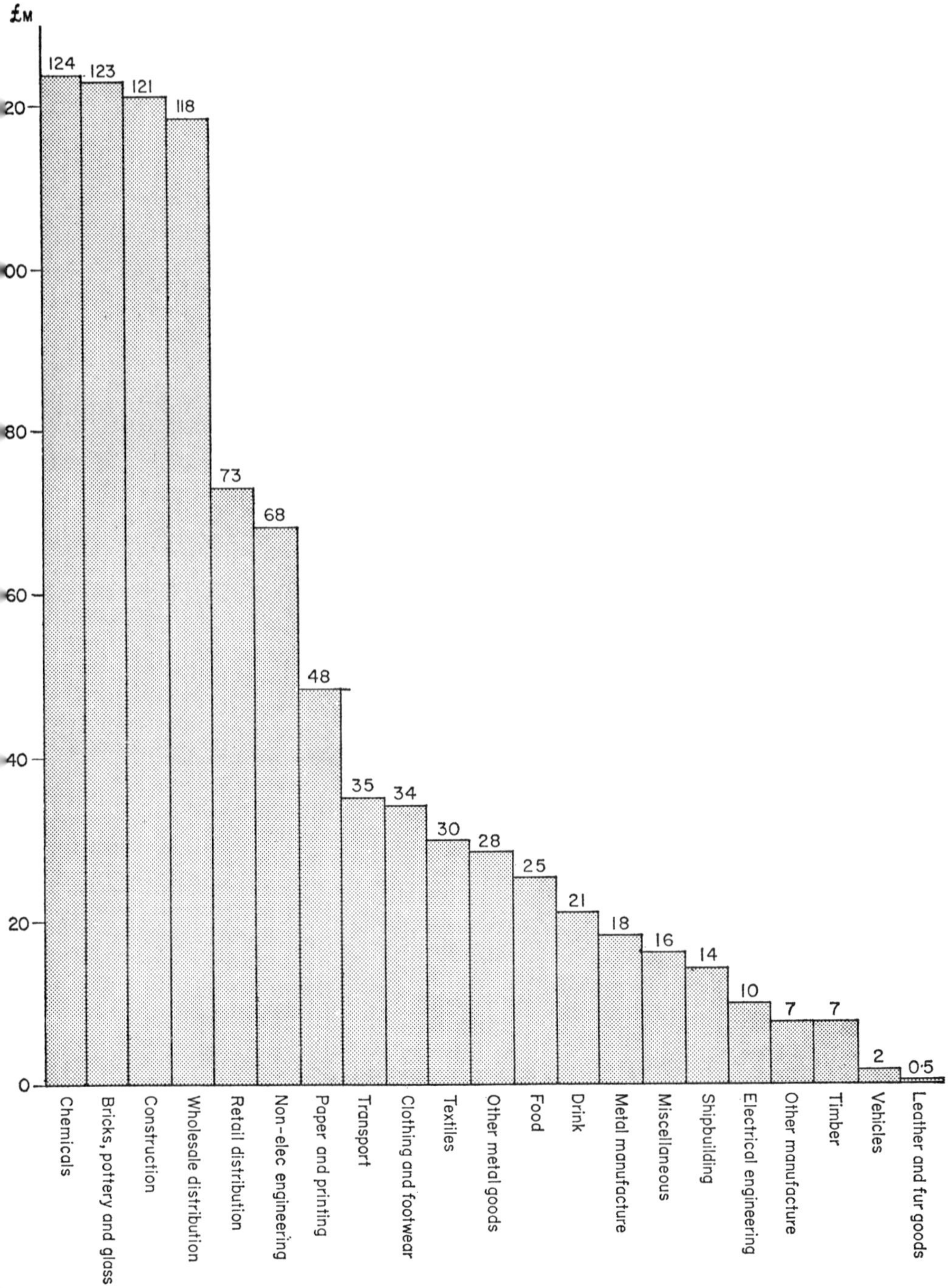

FIGURE 3:2 TOTAL ASSETS OF LARGE PRIVATE COMPANIES BY INDUSTRY, 1966.

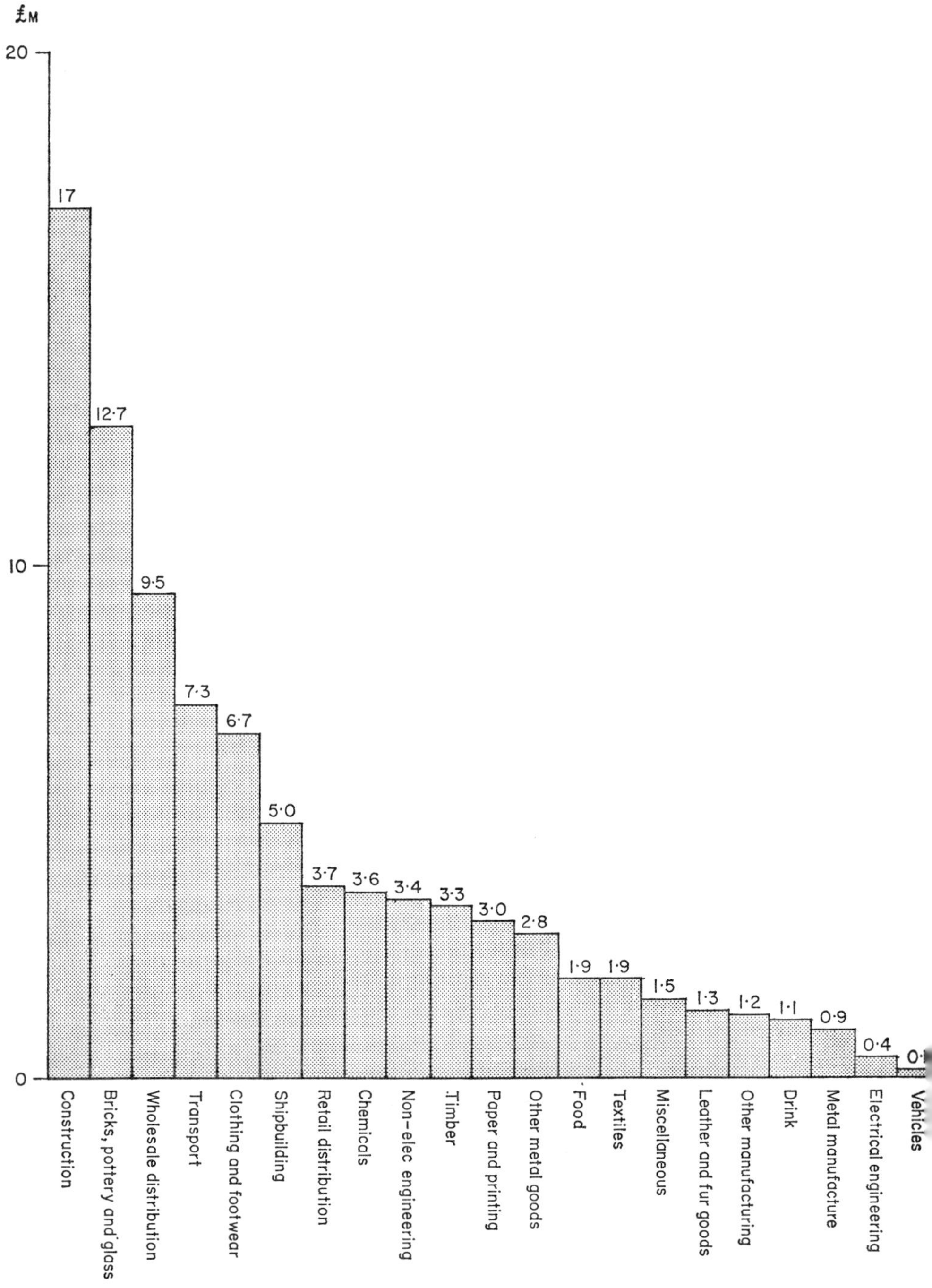

FIGURE 3:3 TOTAL ASSETS OF LARGE PRIVATE COMPANIES AS A PERCENTAGE OF LARGE PUBLIC COMPANIES' TOTAL ASSETS, 1966

—for example, that one sample itself contains more companies in high-return *industries* than does the other. For this reason the analysis needs to be conducted in terms of a comparison between companies within the same industry.

The second possible cause of distortion is differences in relative size—for example, it is possible that the smaller companies can show a high rate of return simply as a result of the efforts of one or two individuals (probably the proprietors) who have not charged at full economic salaries for certain services. For this reason the comparison needs to be on the basis of companies of sufficient size to avoid these exceptional distorting factors associated with small companies.

Finally, the analysis must be on the basis of there being enough companies in each comparison to avoid the outcome's being simply due to chance and the freakish results from one or two companies only.

On these grounds the comparison of rates of return on total assets shown in Figure 3:4 compares large companies in specific industries and excludes all industries where the number of companies was less than five. (This, in practice, has meant omitting the following industries: shipbuilding, vehicles and leather and fur goods.) Also excluded were retail and wholesale distribution since comparison between companies in these industries is not possible without detailed correction of the figures on to a common basis of property ownership. (The return in either of these industries is substantially dependent on how far the companies own rather than rent properties and how far their rentals are geared to current market rates rather than lower rents under long-term leases concluded many years earlier.)

Since the results for individual years may be unrepresentative, the average return over the two years 1966 and 1967 has been calculated. Also in order to give appropriate weighting to the larger companies, the returns given in the tables are weighted in the sense of representing the return which arises from totalling the profits of all the companies and dividing by their total assets.

Results of the comparison

The fifteen industrial groups of quoted and private companies are compared in Figure 3:4. It is seen that the private companies had a higher rate of return in eleven out of the fifteen industry categories considered. The differences are most marked in metal manufacture, food and drink where the returns are respectively 77 per cent, 44 per cent and 43 per cent higher than those of their quoted sector counterparts.

INDUSTRY	Weighted average return on TA%	
	Private companies	Public companies
Food	14.0	9.7
Drink	14.2	9.9
Chemicals	10.1	8.5
Metal manufacture	12.6	7.1
Non-electrical engineering	7.9	8.3
Electrical engineering	6.0	9.9
Other metal goods	13.1	10.5
Textiles	5.5	9.3
Clothing and footwear	10.2	9.3
Bricks, pottery, glass	10.8	10.5
Timber	9.5	8.5
Paper and printing	11.2	8.8
Other manufacturing	13.5	8.8
Construction	8.3	7.7
Transport	6.2	7.9

FIGURE 3:4 WEIGHTED MEAN RETURN ON TOTAL ASSETS, 1966–7

The adverse differences are greatest in textiles and electrical engineering which respectively earned returns of 41 per cent and 39 per cent less than those of public companies. In both cases, however, the industries covered in fact embrace activities with markedly different economic characteristics—for example, the textiles industry ranges from modern synthetic fibre plants to specialist traditional processing of wool, and there is no economic point of comparison between the two. Similarly electrical engineering ranges over the whole range of activities and the major public companies classified under that head (GEC, AEI) have in fact extensive interests both in other industries and outside the UK.

Conclusion

Except on the most detailed and comparable basis, assessment of the efficiency of companies by reference to their rates of return must be regarded with considerable reservations. The comparison used here, however, in terms of return on total assets and by industry groups, excluding industries where there were major problems of accounting comparability, is as accurate as is practically possible from published data. Of the fifteen industry groups compared, the "large" private companies were found to have higher rates of return on total assets in eleven instances (73 per cent). Moreover, the differences were in many cases most marked, and in three cases (metal manufacturing, drink and food) the private sector showed returns of some 43 per cent higher than the quoted.

While there are significant problems of accounting comparability in terms of valuation of assets and reported profitability between the two sectors, there is the strong likelihood that the advantage of minimising company personal tax liability and the absence of shareholder pressure for high reported profits makes private companies substantially understate their profitability. This and the above statistical analysis suggest that there are considerable grounds for arguing that private are more efficient than quoted companies in the size and industry categories in which they overlap. There is, however, no practicable basis on which the performance of the smaller private enterprise (which accounts for 34 per cent of employment) can be compared with public companies since each is clearly specialising in areas in which they do not overlap. They have different comparative advantages, a characteristic which forms the subject of the following chapter.

Chapter Four
The Special Role of The Private Company

The special economic contribution of the private company (and the private sector generally) must be distinguished from the purely statistical analyses of the preceding chapters. The statistics would be an indication of relative importance only if public and private companies were essentially the same in all respects other than size. This is not the case. The two sectors are in fact very different in role and function; hence they are not substitutes to be compared on a purely statistical basis.

Size and efficiency

Historically the larger public companies have typically come into being as a means of bringing together the advantages of size—in marketing, production, research and finance—wherever these were sufficiently large to outweigh the administrative and motivational disadvantages of the relatively large company.

The administrative disadvantages of a large company compared with a number of smaller companies, having the same turnover in aggregate, arise out of the problems of control and communication. This is at its most obvious in, say, a hotel chain. Combining two hotels, which were formerly operated by independent managing proprietors, automatically creates the need for a new layer of control. Additional information is required at the centre in addition to the pre-existing control information, since the performance of the former proprietor (or his replacement) must now be assessed and controlled by the central management. This duplication is essential if central management is not to abdicate control and responsibility; it is not open to it to adopt the role of holding the individual hotels as an investor might hold different shares in his portfolio. This is because in practice central management stands in the role of virtually unlimited liability, since it must meet losses and finance the investment of all the different operations. Unlike the stock market investor it cannot readily dispose of its holding.

A related problem is that costs of control and communication increase more than in proportion to size. For example, one supervisory manager might be able to supervise, say, eight hotels; but as this number gets larger, additional supervisory management will be required. Ultimately the interposition of a further layer of control management concerned with the control of the supervisors becomes necessary. Thus there emerges the characteristic quadruple modern management structure of operating, supervisory, regional (product or division in manufacturing) and board management. In larger companies this frequently extends to a quintuple management structure in that the board will have a central management team of its own reporting on matters of central policy and the performance of other layers of management. Moreover each stage of increased remoteness from day-to-day operations creates a need for more detailed numerical information as a substitute for on-the-spot assessments made by the former proprietor-manager.

Motivating management towards the achievement of good financial performance is a major problem in all substantial companies concerned with their overall financial performance. With salaried management providing the effort and bearing the risks of failure but benefiting little from the financial success of its efficiency or new initiatives there is an inherent contradiction in the divorce of management and proprietorship. Many of the developments of organisation and remuneration in large companies can be seen as an attempt to overcome this contradiction. The commonly used device of breaking the company into cost-and-profit centres and remunerating the manager in charge on the basis of centre results (performance-related remuneration) is in effect an attempt to reproduce some of the conditions of proprietorial management in a large company context. (For further discussion of performance-related remunerations, see *Incentive Payment Systems for Managers* by A J Merrett and M R White (Gower Press, 1969).) This type of substitute for proprietorial management is, however, costly to administer; not only is separate accounting required for each cost centre, but complex and detailed analysis is required to interpret the results and to set standards of performance, since this has to be done at central management level away from the actual local conditions. It may also be questioned whether the outcome is as effective in motivating salaried management as proprietorial investment (*a*) because high marginal rates of taxation break the link between effort and reward and (*b*) because its effective operation depends upon the motivation of *central management:* this itself may not be being held adequately accountable by shareholders where these are merely institutions or small shareholders, rather than active major shareholders with a proprietorial interest in the company.

In certain industries there will, of course, be offsetting advantages to the company. These are characteristically the advantages of:

1 Lower per unit costs
2 Ability to charge higher prices
3 Greater purchasing power

Of these, 1 is clearly an unqualified economic advantage but 2 and 3 may provide zero additional economic benefits to the community. While not necessarily disadvantageous it is hardly possible to argue that there are net economic advantages from greater concentration, eliminating competition and raising prices. In the case of the advantage of the greater purchasing power of retail chains, etc, this is not a net economic benefit to the economy as a whole, but only a transfer of profit from producer to retailer and customer. It does not involve the net increase in economic wealth that would arise from a more efficient use of resources producing more output.

In addition to such situations, in which size confers no overall economic benefit, there are, of course, a considerable number in which companies have grown large for historical reasons—for example, being first in the field—or by accident of acquisition, without additional size being of significant economic advantage. In sum there are a number of grounds for not generally equating size either with scope for greater efficiency or net improvement in economic benefit *to the community*. This, however, is in no way to deprecate the undoubted advantages of size in specific areas of the economy.

Role of the private company

The basic functions of the public and private sectors are set out in Figure 4:1. The function of the public company is in servicing markets and technologies (the size-economic industries) in which the advantages of size outweigh the higher administrative and motivational costs of size. This function, as the table suggests, extends to the large private companies some of which—for example, Pilkingtons, Sainsbury's, Wates and Bamford Excavators, etc—are major companies in their particular industries.

Sole traders partnerships	Small private companies	Large private companies	Public companies
1 Non-scale-economic markets and products		1 Scale-economic markets and products	
2 Maintenance of competition 3 Vehicle for innovation 4 Vehicle for long-term growth			

FIGURE 4:1 ROLE OF THE PRIVATE SECTOR

The *common* functions of the private sector (covering both large and small private companies as well as enterprises working without limited liability) are shown on the left-hand side of the table. Their first common role is in the maintenance of competition both between themselves and, more importantly, with the public companies. The possibility of the limitation of competition (or its direction into channels disadvantageous to the consumer—such as competitive advertising) evidently increases as the number of companies decreases, since the smaller the number of companies the greater is the likelihood of tacit or overt collusion. Moreover, competition between quoted companies can itself be checked simply by a process of acquisition of competitors.

Checks on monopoly situations

However, where competition has been minimised among quoted companies and profitability is tending to increase through monopolistic price increases, it becomes increasingly profitable for private companies to expand and secure a sizeable portion of the market with lower prices. Such a possibility acts as a check upon the abuse of monopolistic power. Moreover, it is far more difficult for the competition of the private company to be eliminated by a process of acquisition. There are obvious reasons for this—principally that the private company does not have publicly traded shares which a competitor can buy up, and tends to comprise a comparatively large number of smaller units where the administrative costs of scale and the time involved would make the policy of checking competition by aquisition quite uneconomic. (The fact that the proprietors are also interested in more than the purely financial benefits provided by their company also makes acquisition considerably more difficult.)

The second general role of the private sector is that of providing a vehicle for innovation in products, marketing and production. In this respect it has been far more important than its relative size would suggest. (See *Sources of Invention* by John Jewkes, David Sawers, and Richard Stillerman, Macmillan & Co Ltd, 1958.) Many innovations require for their success a degree of unfettered dedication and personal drive which it is difficult to reproduce in the confederate power structure found in most relatively large companies. There are a number of well-known examples of technological innovation brought in by individuals operating initially in a small company environment—for example the Polaroid camera and xerography—and, in the context of larger private companies, there is the example of the series of great out-rolling advances in the manufacture of plate glass, culminating in the development of the float process brought about by Pilkingtons. Similar conditions apply where the innovations are more in the nature of commercial and management organisation. Examples of this are the pioneering of supermarket chains in this country by Sainsbury and Tesco (the latter subsequently becoming a public company); and Lansing Bagnall, which still leads the UK in methods of mechanical handling.

These considerations might be generalised into the proposition that it is an important function of the large private company to take the long view and relatively high risks. This is one which the large public company generally finds extremely difficult to undertake on account of the considerable pressure of the stock market for immediate and tangible results in terms of reported profits. Moreover it may well be questioned whether it would be desirable to encourage large public companies to take over more of this function. They are in a position of trust in relation to the shareholders' capital—unlike the private company which is primarily deploying the capital of the management—and the statement that this function was being performed could serve as an excuse for the inefficient and indeed irresponsible use of capital.

Turning now to the role of the smaller enterprise in the private sector this might be generally characterised as supplying those markets in which the economies from large-scale production or marketing are not sufficiently large to outweigh the administrative and motivational costs of size. Whilst it is convenient to talk of industries in general categories, there are, in fact, specific areas within almost every industrial classification where the smaller enterprise is the most efficient unit of activity. For example, the industries and indeed companies classified as engineering are characteristically a conglomeration of economically dissimilar operations. It is significant in this context that the private business (see Chapter 1), accounts for 38 per cent of the total industrial employment.

Other major areas in which the unqouted sector would appear to be at a substantial competitive advantage occur wherever the activity concerned is discontinuous or requires local independence and initiative. This type of situation is characteristic of the construction industry, and here the unquoted sector probably accounts for nearly two thirds of all employment. In this case the operations are geographically highly fragmented and there is a considerable need for independent local management for the efficient provision and control of the many different activities (and indeed industries) which are classified as the construction industry.

Finally, reference should be made to the financial, professional and other services which account for a large section of the unquoted sector. It is in these activities that the advantages of size are least significant and the advantages of the highly motivated individual able to act on personal initiative are of the greatest importance.

Conclusions

The public and large private companies have the common function of serving the "scale-economic" markets in which production and marketing economies outweigh the administrative and motivational costs of size. The whole of the unquoted sector, however, has the common and vitally important function of:

1 Maintaining competition in the industry as a whole
2 Providing a vehicle for innovation and serving the myriad and diverse markets which are not scale-economic

In addition to terminal markets, such as retailing and professional services this function covers a wide range of activities supplying special component, and services to the larger public and private companies.

Part Two

Tax and the Private Company

Chapter Five

Tax Burden of The Private Company

The privately controlled company has been seen to play a special and important part in the efficient running of the economy. Moreover, it is clear that it is the combination of ownership and control which gives such companies the qualities required for this role. Ownership must imply the possession, directly or indirectly, of wealth, while one of the most consistent trends in fiscal policy throughout Europe and the English-speaking world, is the attempt to restrict the accumulation of wealth and to break up existing accumulations. This chapter first briefly surveys the taxes imposed on wealth in the UK. It then surveys the probable impact of these taxes in the future—an impact which is likely to be very different from in the past, given the creation of additional taxes on wealth and legislation against many of the major devices for tax minimisation throughout the 1960s.

Taxes on wealth

The various taxes on wealth and their estimated yields for 1970–1 are shown in Figure 5:1. The total revenue of £840M may be compared with the £277M of revenue from surtax and the £5653M from income tax. It is seen from the table that estate duties produce £371M or 44 per cent of the total and this is nearly two and a half times the yield of capital gains tax. Estate duties are therefore the principal tax on wealth.

Estate duty law is based on the Finance Act 1894 as amended by many subsequent Acts. The duty is a tax on property "passing" on the death of individuals, but the definition of "passing" has been substantially extended by the legislation in the 1950s and 1960s to cover virtually the whole of any

	Estimated yield 1970–1 £m
Estate duty	371
Capital gains tax	150
Stamp duties	119
Additional income and surtax on investment compared with earned income[1]	200
TOTAL	840

FIGURE 5:1 WEALTH TAXES
Sources: Financial Statement 1970–1
[1]Written Parliamentary Answer, 18 April 1967

property in which individuals had any beneficial interest. It has, for example, by the Finance Act 1969, been extended to beneficiaries of trusts, by there being deemed to pass on death that part of the trust property which is regarded as representing his beneficial interest (based on his receipts from the trust). Its jurisdiction covers property situated in Great Britain and indeed property outside Great Britain unless its passing is governed by foreign law and the deceased either dies domiciled outside of Great Britain or was so

Estate £			Slice rate %	Total rate %
0	—	10 000	Nil	0
10 000	—	17 500	25	10.7
17 500	—	30 000	30	18.7
30 000	—	40 000	45	25.3
40 000	—	80 000	60	42.7
80 000	—	150 000	65	53.1
150 000	—	300 000	70	61.5
300 000	—	500 000	75	66.9
500 000	—	750 000	80	71.3
750 000	—	1 000 000	85	74.7
1 000 000	—	2 000 000	85	80.0

FIGURE 5:2 ESTATE DUTIES, 1969–70

domiciled at the time of making the legal instrument governing the passing of the property. In intent, therefore, estate duty is meant to be applicable to everyone having domicile in the UK.

The rates of estate duty payable in the year 1969–70 are shown in Figure 5:2. These are seen to be extremely high, with the total rate rising from 53.1 per cent on an estate of £150 000 to 80 per cent on an estate of £2M. (Moreover, as will be seen below, the rates of tax payable at death have been increased dramatically by the imposition of capital gains tax, for property passing at death is deemed to have been disposed of for capital gains tax purposes.)

A point of considerable importance as a precedent is the fact that agricultural land and industrial buildings, machinery and plant, where this is part of the estate of "the person carrying on the business," is given a 45 per cent reduction in estate duty. However, in order to take advantage of this abatement it is of critical importance both:

1 That the individual continues to "carry on the business"
2 That his holding is sufficiently large to prevent the business from being threatened by the levying of estate duties on the estates of *other* shareholders who cannot claim this abatement

In effect this provision creates the situation that any substantial reliance on external equity finance from a few private individuals increases the vulnerability of the business to estate duties levied on those individuals; while a stock market quotation for the shares increases the vulnerability of the proprietor's control of the business since this is likely to cause him to fall out of the classification "the person carrying on the business" for purposes of the abatement provision.

Discretionary trusts

The two major forms of avoidance of estate duty have been the discretionary trust and gifts *inter vivos*. Discretionary trusts are settlements by which individuals could be beneficiaries of the wealth of a trust without having any legal claim to ownership and hence neither they nor the trust having any liability to estate duty. The loophole was effectively closed by the Finance Acts of 1965 and 1969. The Act of 1965 made such trusts subject to capital gains tax on "deemed" realisations of the underlying assets—that is, made them subject to capital gains tax on the accrued capital gains insofar as these capital gains had not been realised and therefore already subjected to capital gains tax. By the Finance Act of 1969 a capital value was imputed to the benefits received under a discretionary trust and this capital value taken into account as part of the beneficiary's estate on death, hence making the wealth subject to estate duties.

Gifts *inter vivos*

Gifts *inter vivos* (gifts made in the donor's lifetime) were exempt from estate duties prior to the 1968 Finance Act if the gifts were made more than five years before death. Under the 1968 Act, however, estate duties were made payable on gifts made up to seven years before death, with 85 per cent of the gift being taken into the estate for duty purposes when death occurred in the fifth year after the gift, 70 per cent in the sixth year, and 40 per cent in the seventh year after the gift. (These abatement provisions formerly applied to the third, fourth and fifth years.)

This extension to seven years of the period before death, during which gifts are treated as part of the estate, must be seen as part of a progressive move towards a gifts tax. It seems probable that this will ultimately be along the lines of that of the United States, which effectively taxes gifts on a cumulative basis at three-quarters of estate duty rates. It might be noted, however, that the maximum rates of estate duty in the United States are 77 per cent but are subject to a "marital deduction" under which the descendant can pass as much as one-half of his estate to his surviving spouse tax free and that, even without this abatement, the US rate of estate tax is 51 per cent on estates of £2.06M at which the UK rate of tax becomes 80 per cent.

With enactment of a full-scale gifts tax, the only remaining means of avoiding estate duty would be for the individual to change his domicile. Such a change of domicile would necessitate the individual's spending less than three months a year in the UK and would inevitably result in a substantial impairment of an individual's control of any substantial private company. It would certainly preclude that major involvement in the day-to-day running of the company which has been seen to be an important factor giving rise to the flexibility and expansionist character of these companies.

In the longer term it is also a remote possibility that even change of domicile will allow the passing of an estate without tax to other UK residents who might maintain effective control. The extension of estate duty to cover gifts would probably follow the US example and impose the liability to tax on the recipient insofar as it was not met by the donor. Under these conditions there would appear to be no method whatever that would then permit the preservation of control (by ownership) of a substantial private company by individuals domiciled in the UK.

Capital gains tax

Capital gains tax was seen from Figure 5:1 to give a yield of £150M or about 18 per cent of all taxes on wealth. The first capital gains tax was introduced by a Conservative administration and embodied in the Finance Act of 1962. This taxed short-term capital gains (those realised within six months) as income. While this set the general principle of taxation of capital gains, such taxation was greatly extended by the last Labour Government's Finance Act of 1965, which imposed a long-term capital gains tax of 30 per cent on capital gains realised after more than one year. (The same Act allows the alternative of including one half of such capital gains as taxable income.)

The capital gains tax makes no allowance for the extent to which the capital appreciation being taxed is purely inflationary, with no underlying growth in the real value of the underlying assets. On the other hand, unlike taxes on income, it is a tax which is delayed until actual realisation of the assets. The most revealing method of assessing its effective impact is to consider what rate of tax paid each year on the accrued capital gains *in real terms*—that is, after allowing for inflation—would be equivalent to this deferred capital gains tax liability on realised capital gains in money terms. This is a complex calculation (see "The Capital Gains Tax," by A J Merrett, *Lloyds Bank Review*, August 1965), but the results may be summarised as follows. Inflation in the UK in terms of the retail price index proceeds at some 3½ per cent a year while the rate of appreciation of the Financial Times 500 index over the seven years from 1962 to 1969 was 5.2 per cent a year. The real increase in the capital value of shares is therefore approximately 1.7 per cent a year. Assuming the shares are held on average for seven years, the capital gains tax on the appreciation in money terms (for example the 5.2 per cent a year) is equivalent to a tax of 72 per cent levied each year on the 1.7 per cent appreciation in real terms. In other words, under the present inflationary conditions the tax payer is effectively paying over 72 per cent of his real capital gains in taxation.

Differential taxation of unearned income

The differential taxation of unearned income arises from the fact that such income does not qualify for earned income relief. This relief takes the form of excluding two-ninths of the first £4005 and one-ninth of the next

£5940 of earned income from liability to income tax and surtax. Effectively, therefore, there is a higher rate of tax on investment compared with earned income, and this can reasonably be regarded as taxation of capital. This differential taxation was estimated in 1967 to produce some £200M of tax revenues. Currently it is probably nearer to £250M and is therefore the second largest form of taxation on wealth after estate duties.

The differential taxation of unearned income is of particular importance in the context of proprietorially owned companies since it is this rate of tax that will fall upon any dividends paid by the company to the proprietors. Given that the latter will typically be in receipt of earned income from their managerial functions in these companies and that this will account for between £8000 and £10 000 of income, the full rigours of the marginal rate of tax on unearned income above this level will fall upon dividends paid. This will make the average tax rate on dividends close to the highest rate of income tax and surtax—that is $91\frac{1}{4}$ per cent. In this situation £1000 of taxation on wealth that had to be met by increased dividends would require £11 428 of additional dividends. These in their turn would require nearly £21 000 of pre-corporation tax profits to replace the outflow of cash from the company.

Long-term impact of current taxes on wealth

The long-term impact of the increased burden of taxation on wealth will be gradual but will nevertheless bring about a basic change in the structure of private control of UK companies. This basic change arises from the relative magnitude of taxes that will have to be paid. Some assessment of this can be arrived at by considering the proportion of an initial holding of a company's shares that would need to be sold in order to meet such taxes.

In the not untypical case of a company which is growing at a rate of around 5 per cent a year in terms of capital employed and sales, the position might be that retained earnings (equal to 5 per cent, say, of the company's equity capital) provides the required increase in equity, while debt capital contributes the remainder. (The return on equity capital of "large" private companies was 8.2 per cent in 1962 while the proportion retained was 58 per cent. Hence the assumption of a 5 per cent growth rate financed by retentions can be taken as fairly realistic.) In this situation the shares of the company would probably be regarded as having increased in value by 5 per cent every year and at death capital gains tax would be payable on this capital appreciation while estate duties would be levied on the balance of the estate.

Figure 5:3 illustrates the combined rates of capital gains and estate duties which would be payable on various levels of estate where the accumulation of capital gains had continued over twenty years, assuming no intermediate realisation of the asset had given rise to an earlier capital gains tax liability. It is seen from the table that the effect of the imposition of a capital gains tax liability on top of estate duties is to bring about a substantial increase in the total rate of tax payable.

Estate £	Slice rate %	Total rate %	Total rate and capital gains tax %
0 — 10 000	nil	0	18.3
10 000 — 17 500	25	10.7	27.0
17 500 — 30 000	30	18.7	33.6
30 000 — 40 000	45	25.3	39.1
40 000 — 80 000	60	42.7	53.2
80 000 — 150 000	65	53.1	61.7
150 000 — 300 000	70	61.5	68.6
300 000 — 500 000	75	66.9	73.0
500 000 — 750 000	80	71.3	76.6
750 000 — 1 000 000	85	74.7	79.3
1 000 000 — 2 000 000	85	80.0	83.7

FIGURE 5:3 CAPITAL GAINS TAX AND ESTATE DUTIES

Moreover this increase in tax rates is very much concentrated in the lower levels of estates. For example, it is seen that over a twenty-year period of accumulated capital gains, the effect of capital gains tax is to raise the total taxes paid on an estate of £30 000 from 18.7 per cent to 33.6 per cent—a near doubling. In the case of an estate of £80 000 the effect of the capital gains tax is to raise the overall taxes payable on death from 42.7 per cent to 53.2 per cent. At the 80 per cent upper limit of estate duties, the effect is to increase the overall taxes paid to 83.7 per cent, an increase of nearly 4 percentage points. Nevertheless this is effectively cutting the estate remaining after death duties by nearly one-fifth; from 20 per cent to 16.3 per cent.

The evident conclusion is therefore that the imposition of capital gains tax on deemed disposals at death effectively amounts to a massive increase in death duties at the lower end of the estate duty scale with the result that even relatively modest estates are now subject to very high rates of tax which effectively begin at 27 per cent.

The effect of taxation would be even more severe if the shares were held in the form of a trust. In this case the deemed realisation every fifteen years in respect of capital gains held in trust would result in the trust's having to meet a capital gains tax liability equal to 15 per cent of the value of its assets every fifteen years. In addition it would have estate duties levied on the beneficial interest, actual or imputed, of the beneficiaries of the trust. Hence the result is somewhat more severe than that indicated in Figure 5:3.

Four methods of meeting tax liability

Essentially the capital gains and estate duty liability (if made technically unavoidable) could only be met by one of the following methods:

1. By the proprietor's reducing consumption or by savings out of earned income
2. By distributions and cutting back on the growth of the company
3. By disposal of most of the equity capital by obtaining a quotation or a merger
4. By liquidating the business

These possibilities are best looked at in the context of a specific example.

Consider the case of a company the whole of whose share capital (valued at £100 000 in 1965, when capital gains tax was introduced) is owned by its managing director, who has an income from employment and dividends of £10 000 a year. Along the lines of the previous example, this company would be earning around 8 per cent net of tax on its equity capital and growing at around 5 per cent a year from its retentions. Assuming death is likely to occur twenty years after 1965, the company at that time would probably be valued at around £266 000. Capital gains tax would therefore be payable on the £166 000 capital appreciation, and with exemption of the first £5000 of gains the capital gains tax liability would be £48 300. Estate duty would then be payable on the balance of the estate, namely £217 700. Assuming this to be the whole of the estate, this tax would be approximately £126 620 making a total tax liability of £174 920.

Considering now the methods of meeting this liability, the first possibility (that of meeting liability out of savings) could only be of marginal usefulness. Given that the proprietor will have an income of around £10 000 gross (roughly £6000 net) the maximum likely saving is, say, £1000 a year, which invested in endowment policies might accumulate to some £33 000 at the end of the twenty years. Even if entirely free of estate duty and capital gains tax this would meet less than one-fifth of tax liability. Moreover, although the actual tax position of insurance policy premiums and ultimate endowments is complex, the general tendency of estate duty legislation (and certainly the logic of making estate duty fully unavoidable) is to make them fully subject to estate duty. In this event the £33 000 would be subject to 70 per cent estate duty.

Meeting the liability out of savings therefore would at best make at a modest contribution to total taxes payable at death; but with the endowment itself assessed to estate duty this possibility would be of negligible usefulness. Under present conditions, then, savings could at best be regarded as a means of meeting only the capital gains tax liability which would arise either at death or with the transfer of shares as a gift.

The second possibility, that of additional dividends from the company, would also be of only marginal usefulness in meeting future capital gains and estate duty liabilities since the additional distribution would be subject to the full rates of tax on unearned income and this would approach 91¼ per cent, given the existing £10 000 of income being received by the proprietor. Moreover, it would evidently eliminate the scope for retentions by the company and hence eliminate its capacity for growth, jeopardising its long-term viability as it proves unable to meet the growing requirements of its customers.

It should be noted that the conclusions as regards the first and second possibilities apply even more strongly in the case of larger companies. For example, in the case of a company with a valuation of £200 000, the increasing marginal rates of tax on earned and unearned income make it even more impractical for the proprietor to meet the larger liability to estate duty and capital gains tax out of savings or additional dividends.

The practicability of the third possibility—that of disposal of the shares—will depend on whether the company is sufficiently large for a flotation or to be of interest to a quoted company. The minimum size limit for a quotation is £100 000 of pre-tax profits (implying an equity valuation of more than £0.5M) while the size limit for a worth-while merger would probably be profits of around £50 000 or more. It was seen in Chapter 2 (Figure 2:5) however, that only 2000 odd of the 291 600 unquoted companies had profits in excess of £50 000. It must therefore be concluded that the option of a quotation or a merger is open only to a tiny faction of all the private companies.

In practical terms it is also highly improbable that a significant proportion of these "unmarriageable" and "non-floatable" companies could sell the requisite proportion of their equity capital even to institutions such as the ICFC and IEDITH. There are two reasons for this. The first is quite simply that the cost of administering any minority interest in companies of this size would in most cases be uneconomic. Second, any institution taking a stake in the company would in practice be faced with the ultimate option either of purchasing the bulk of the equity capital as successive demands for capital gains tax and estate duties necessitate further disposals by existing shareholders, hence making it a subsidiary, or alternatively of acquiescing in the company's being closed down to enable shareholders to realise their assets.

It is hardly conceivable that any government institution would contemplate a situation in which it undertook full responsibility for literally tens of thousands of independent subsidiary companies. Quite apart from the immense administrative costs involved in any such exercise, it would be involved in the well-nigh infinite variety of small local management problems that make acquisition of such small companies unattractive to existing quoted companies. It follows by elimination, therefore, that it is the fourth possibility—that of liquidation—which would have to be accepted by private companies that were not small enough to avoid estate duties—that is, were less than £10 000 in value—or large enough to obtain a quotation or merger with an existing quoted company.

The imposition of a wealth tax would involve much the same consequences, but since this is a tax that could not even be deferred, it would greatly accelerate the process. It was seen that even for the smaller company, the savings of the proprietor (if in a form free from estate duty) would at best be sufficient to meet only the future capital gains tax liability. An annual wealth tax of 1 per cent on shareholders, however, could not in the great majority of cases even be met by the distribution of the whole of the company's profits as dividends. Consider, for example, the case in which the value of the shares for wealth tax purposes is taken as equal to the value of the company's equity assets (that is shareholder's capital in the company). The net of corporation tax earnings on such assets is normally in the range of 8 to 10 per cent.

Given then that any distribution would be subject to the massive rates of marginal taxation imposed on unearned income (this would certainly be 91¼ per cent in the case of the working proprietor with £10 000 of earned income), the shareholders would receive a dividend net of income tax and surtax which was less than 1 per cent of equity assets even if the whole of the company's net of tax profits were distributed as dividends. Hence wherever the valuation of the shares is taken as close to equity assets even a total distribution of profits would not leave sufficient in the hands of shareholders net of tax to meet even a 1 per cent wealth tax liability. Moreover the outcome for the company of such distributions would in any case be extremely serious since the whole of its capacity for further equity financing through retained earnings would have been eliminated. In the majority of cases this would also effectively eliminate the capacity of the company for further growth.

It is, of course, arguable that the wealth tax could take the form of being itself allowable against income tax and surtax, as in the case of West Germany. But in this eventuality its net yield would make it uneconomic in the context of the high rates of personal taxation applicable in the UK. Consider, for example, the case of an individual paying £1000 in wealth tax, where such a tax is levied at a rate of 1 per cent on the amount by which his net wealth exceeded £20 000. Such an individual by definition must have wealth of £120 000, and income from this (in conjunction with a modest amount of earned income) would result in his paying the highest rates of income tax and surtax on income. If the £10 000 wealth tax were then allowed against such taxes on income, the result would be that the Revenue would receive £10 000 of wealth tax while losing £9125 of income tax and surtax, making the net amount of tax raised only £875. In other words the net yield of the tax (even before the costs of collection) would be only 8.75 per cent of its nominal amount.

Overseas taxation of wealth

The forms of wealth taxation employed in other industrialised countries are of relevance in assessing proposals for similar taxation on wealth in the UK in that they are indicative of foreign experience and are also factors influencing the efficiency of economies with which the UK, through its international trade, is in competition. The last consideration is referred to in the next chapter, while we are here concerned with the first issue of international comparisons and experience.

International comparisons are inevitably difficult since the actual tax practice will turn upon detailed legislation as well as general principles and nominal rates of tax. Figure 5:4, however, provides a broad indication of comparative taxation of wealth in the main developed European countries.

Since wealth taxation, however, cannot be looked at in isolation, the table also covers death duties and rates of income tax.

Considering estate duties first, the first two columns of the table relate to the typical distinction made by the Continental European (and the US) legislatures between estates passing to close relations of the deceased and estates passing to outsiders. It is seen that UK death duties, which make no such distinction, are higher than the highest applicable even to outsiders. With the exception of Belgium at 75 per cent and Sweden at 65 per cent, the UK rate of 80 per cent is seen to be at least a third higher than in the other countries given in the table.

Even this, however, considerably understates the comparative scale of UK death duties since obviously the great bulk of estates are left to close relatives. Hence it is the first column (applicable to close relations) that should form the basis of the comparison. It is seen from this column that the UK rate of death duties is substantially more than twice as high as the other rates given in the table, with the exception of Sweden at 60 per cent.

Consider now the effective maximum rates of income tax given in the last but one column of the table. The UK maximum effective tax rate of 91.25 per cent is seen to be more than 10 percentage points higher than that of the highest other country in the table (France at 80.76 per cent) and 20 percentage points higher than the Netherlands at 70.5 per cent. Characteristically it is about 30 percentage points higher than in other European countries. A further consideration is that in most of the countries shown in the table, there is a statutory limit to the total of income and wealth taxes. In West Germany, where this is not so, wealth tax is allowed as a deduction against income tax. Hence the situation which would apply in the UK, of taxes constituting more than 100 per cent of income, could not arise.

Essentially, therefore, the UK's existing rates of taxation are massively high compared with other industrialised countries both as regards death duties and taxes on income.

Conclusion

Taxes on wealth were expected to amount to £840M in 1970–1 and of this estate duties accounted for 44 per cent. Starting at 10.7 per cent on estates of £17 500, estate duties rise to 53.1 per cent at £150 000 and run at a maximum rate of 80 per cent. These rates are generally more than twice as high as those in Europe and double the effective rates imposed in the United States. Capital gains tax levied on deemed disposals at death is a further substantial

	Maximum marginal rate of estate duty (%)		Marginal rate of wealth tax (%)	Maximum rate of income tax (%)	
	Close relations	Outsiders		Marginal	Statutory average[1]
Austria	15.0	60.0	0.76[2]	68.12	57.2
Belgium	17.0[3]	75.0[3]	—	66.0[4]	50.0
Denmark	13.0[3]	60.0[5]	1.2	45.0[4]	(80.0)
Finland	11.0[3]	55.0[3]	2.2	53.0[4]	(70.0)
France	20.0[3]	60.0[3]	—	80.76[6]	—
W Germany	15.0[3]	60.0[3]	1.0[7]	54.59[4]	—
Netherlands	17.0[3]	54.0[3]	.06	70.5	(80.0)
Norway	35.0[3]	60.0[3]	1.75	50.0[4]	(80.0)
Sweden	60.0[3]	65.0[3]	1.80	65.0[4]	(80.0)
UK	80.0	80.0	—	91.25	—

FIGURE 5:4 COMPARATIVE TAXES ON WEALTH AND INCOME, 1970

Source: Taxation in Western Europe 1968 (CBI)

Notes

1 Figures in brackets refer to maximum total average income tax plus wealth tax: unbracketed figures are maximum average rates for income tax only

2 Plus 1 per cent tax on real property with value exceeding $100 000

3 Also for gifts *inter vivos*

4 Plus local income tax: Belgium (up to 6 per cent), Denmark (10–20 per cent, Church tax 3–6 per cent) Finland (9–18 per cent, Church tax 1–2 per cent), W Germany (Church tax 10 per cent surcharge), Norway (16–19 per cent), Sweden (about 19 per cent)

5 Gifts *inter vivos* are taxed as income

6 Including 15 per cent surcharge on the tax bill and 6 per cent complementary tax

7 Also Equalisation of Burdens Property Contribution of 50 per cent payable on all property owned on 21 June 1948. The tax is to be discharged over thirty years

escalation of these rates and raises the taxes payable on death from 10.7 per cent to 27.0 per cent on estates as small as £17 500, and at £150 000 raises the rate from 53.1 per cent to 61.7 per cent.

In the particular case with which we are concerned—that of the proprietorially-owned private company—the owners of the companies will invariably be in receipt of substantial earned income, with the result that unearned income in the shape of dividends will tend to suffer extremely high rates of income tax and surtax. Given this, wherever the combined rate of capital gains and death duties reached around 40 per cent (on estates of £40 000), the liability could only be met out of these assets by liquidation or sale. Sale of the company would only be open to less than 1 per cent of the private companies which are in the size bracket capable of flotation or being of interest to existing quoted companies. Because of the unmarketable nature of minority interests in private companies insufficiently large for flotation, these companies, if existing tax rates were rigidly enforced, would be obliged to meet their liability in the only way possible—by going into liquidation.

The effect of imposition of a wealth tax on top of this existing burden of taxes would be dramatic acceleration of the process. Total distribution of all profits would not provide sufficient net of tax to meet even a 1 per cent wealth tax. The impact would therefore be immediate and particularly severe in the case of "non-floatable" unquoted companies in the process of growth and requiring substantial ploughback of profits. These would in fact be effectively precluded from further growth.

Chapter Six
Cost-Benefit Analysis of Increased Taxation

Proposals for modifying the system of taxation are in principle no different from proposals to modify, say, the road or railway system. Each involves both costs and benefits to society, and its justification must be in terms of the latter exceeding the former. This chapter attempts such a cost benefit analysis of the effects of modifying the fiscal system to impose greater taxation on wealth in the form of a wealth tax or gifts tax based on estate duties.

Costs: increase in prices

It was argued in the previous chapter that rendering estate duties unavoidable or imposing a wealth tax would necessitate private companies subject to such a tax choosing ultimately between a public quotation, an amalgamation or going into liquidation. The following estimate of economic costs relates to the situation in which either estate duty is made unavoidable or a wealth tax of 1 per cent or more is imposed on wealth of £100 000 or more.

It is clear at the outset that no precise estimate can be made of a change as basic as the virtual elimination from the economy of the bulk of the private companies. The best that can be attempted is an indication of the possible orders of magnitude of the costs involved and, insofar as these seem to be substantial, of the further need for empirical research before these major changes are allowed to come into being.

The first basic effect of elimination of private companies would be an increase in the price level, as services which they formerly provided were taken over by quoted companies. It was argued in Chapter 4 that private companies have a range of special functions in the economy. These functions enable them to perform a certain range of activities more efficiently and at a lower level of unit costs. This contention was supported by the statistical analysis of Chapter 3 as regards the "large" private companies.

The size of this cost advantage could be gauged from a comparative survey of the prices of services and products provided by private compared with public companies in the particular areas in which private companies are principally established. While it can be no more than a guess based upon ordinary business experience, it is unlikely that the public companies would be found to be charging less than 3 per cent above the prices of private companies in comparable situations. In situations of no direct comparability (beause of differences in the product or service) a corresponding differential of value in favour of the private companies is likely to be found. (A common-sense argument in support of such a differential is that any figure lower than 3 per cent would enable the private companies to be driven out by the public companies, given that the latter have considerably greater financial resources.)

The total turnover of the private companies might be estimated at about £11 000M in 1970 (by grossing up the profit figures of Chapter 2). An overall 3 per cent increase in the costs of providing this turnover by public companies would suggest an overall cost in terms of increased prices of £330M a year.

Costs: export of income and capital

The second major category of costs to be taken into account is the inevitable attempt by those subject to heavy wealth tax to take their estates out of the scope of UK taxation by changing their domicile. Under present tax legislation a change of domicile and disposition of the property by a will or settlement governed by a foreign tax jurisdiction would be sufficient to take the estate out of the net of UK estate duty. In this eventuality, the UK would loose surtax and capital gains imposed upon the individual in question, and in addition would suffer the drain on its balance of payments as the income is remitted to the former UK tax payer's foreign domicile. Moreover, the individual is also likely to export some if not all of his capital.

The possible cost of this export of income and capital is difficult to quantify realistically even in orders of magnitude since the avoidance of estate duties by gifts *inter vivos*, etc, makes the existing Inland Revenue statistics on wealth based on estate duty data extremely unreliable. Even taking the Inland Revenue estimates as reliable, however, in 1968 there were 180 000 individuals in the UK with wealth in excess of £50 000 and this wealth in total had a valuation of £21 000M (Inland Revenue Statistics 1970.) If only 1 per cent of the 180 000 such individuals emigrated as a result of a wealth tax or general imposition of estate duties, the annual economic cost would be £210M in foreign exchange if all of their capital was exported. Given the magnitude of the tax burden involved and the extent to which it would exceed that of alternative domiciles open to the relatively wealthy, additional emigration of at least 2 per cent a year would seem the minimum that could reasonably be expected. The cost of this in capital exports (allowing for some capital being retained in the UK) might be put at around £350M a year.

Costs: administration of wealth tax

The third category of costs would be that of administration of the wealth tax or the strengthening of estate duties. This again is extremely difficult to estimate given that the precise methods and scope of these tax changes have not been fully specified. Substantial costs associated with the collection of a wealth tax would certainly be unavoidable given the complex problems of valuation that would be involved. On present evidence, it would seem unlikely that the cost would be less than the £30M a year estimated by the Confederation of British Industries.

Figure 6:1 brings together these rough orders of magnitude of the possible cost of additional taxation of wealth. It is seen that the total is some £710M.

	Possible cost of additional wealth tax
	£m
Higher costs, etc, from elimination of unquoted companies	330
Export of capital[1]	350
Administrative costs ot Inland Revenue	30
TOTAL	710

FIGURE 6:1 COST OF ADDITIONAL TAXATION

[1] This is taken as having an economic cost to the community of at least equal to its nominal value. Given the sacrifice of economic growth that has occurred to conserve foreign exchange it is almost certainly a substantial underestimate

It must be stressed again at this point that the above figures are nothing more than orders of magnitude of the possible costs involved. With the scanty information currently available, it is open to argument that the actual costs could lie within ± 50 per cent of these figures. Even at £400M a year, however, this would represent some £16 a year for each member of the working population.

Two further important levels of cost should also be taken into account. The first is that which arises from the fact that the same forces eliminating proprietorial management in private companies would also eliminate that element of proprietorial management that continues to exist in public companies. The individuals controlling or partially controlling public companies through the direct or indirect possession of wealth would be subject to the same demands for tax revenues as those with similar interests in the private companies. While in the case of individuals with proprietorial interests in public companies the problem of realising the shares and meeting the tax demands would be greatly facilitated by the fact that the shares are quoted, the outcome would inevitably be an erosion of proprietorial control and involvement in these companies. The costs of this in terms of the progressive erosion of efficiency would require a separate study.

The second major but unquantifiable factor is the loss of the contribution of the private company to competitiveness and innovation. It is undoubtedly true that the establishment and growth of private companies is an important influence in preserving competition and choice, and similarly that private companies have been an important influence in innovation both in products and technology. These factors were considered in Chapter 4. The magnitude of the losses under this heading from elimination of the private company, while by their nature unquantifiable may be very substantial indeed.

Benefits: income for welfare expenditure

As has been seen, the ultimate economic cost of increased taxation of wealth is likely to be very considerable in terms of reduced efficiency and higher costs. This need not be a conclusive objection: consideration must be given to the social benefits that might count as an offset to such cost. The social benefits which are commonly thought of as arising from greater taxation of wealth can be divided into two categories—those of welfare and those of social values.

The welfare argument turns upon the same reasoning used in support of progressive taxation of income: namely that these taxes could be used to assist lower income groups and that the value to them of such assistance is greater than the sacrifices imposed upon the upper income groups who are paying the taxes. (This is the classical argument relating to the diminishing marginal utility of income. It is analysed in some detail in: *The Uneasy Case for Progressive Taxation* by Walter D Blum and Harry Kalven, University of Chicago Press.) The presupposition of this argument as applied to taxation of wealth is that tax revenues from wealth could be used for greater old age pensions, better hospitals, etc. Indeed the assumption that this is the case—or alternatively that higher taxation of wealth would enable lower taxation of income—accounts for the widespread political support for higher taxation of wealth.

It is unquestionably true, however, that this welfare argument for heavier taxation has no material economic validity. That this is the case is an elementary point of economic analysis; but, since the fallacy of equating tax revenues from wealth with scope for greater consumption is so widespread, it is worth while considering it in a little more detail. Resources for greater welfare expenditure or reduced taxation on income can only be provided by reducing existing claims on the nation's resources. These existing claims are those of personal consumption, state spending (including old age pensions and nationalised industries' spending) and private investment. If greater resources are to be found for greater state spending (while other forms of state spending are not to be changed) they can only be provided by reducing either total consumption or private capital investment.

Taxation on income normally does force the taxpayer to reduce his consumption, and therefore releases resources which can be used by the government to increase state spending. It is, however, characteristic of taxpayers with substantial wealth—for example, wealth in excess of £50 000—and particularly when such wealth is typically accompanied by a substantial level of earned income out of which the individual meets his existing consumption—that the taxpayer's level of consumption will not be influenced to any significant degree by taxes on wealth. The situation will simply be that the taxes on wealth—capital gains or estate duties—will be met by selling assets (the shares or property, etc) which represent the wealth in question, or by reducing saving out of income. Such sales of assets or reductions in savings do not reduce the claims on the national resources since they do not involve reductions either in consumption or private investment.

It is possible that very heavy taxation of *moderate* levels of wealth will ultimately have an effect upon consumption, but taxation on relatively *large amounts* of wealth will not have any significant effect of this kind.

This conclusion is in fact accepted in the Labour Party document *Labour's Economic Strategy*. It then qualifies this, however, by arguing that the taxation of wealth would nevertheless enable a reduction in the cost of servicing the National Debt. This possibility is mentioned without reference to its economic advantages to the economy—the implication from a simple reading of the statement is that £1M raised in taxation on wealth would save the community £80 000, say, representing the cost of servicing £1M of the National Debt at an 8 per cent interest rate. That this is not the case can be seen from the following.

Consider first the simplest case in which the government needs to redeem £1M of the National Debt and had planned to do so by issuing a further £1M of new debt in order to find £1M required to pay off the old. As an alternative to this policy it issues no additional new debt but simply imposes a wealth tax which provides £1M of cash with which to redeem the £1M of Government Securities which are now due for redemption. For simplicity of calculation it is assumed that the £1M of taxes is raised from the individual who held £1M of Government Securities that were due for redemption in that year.

In this situation the government appears to avoid having to issue £1M of new debt and to make an interest saving of £80 000. The bulk of this economy, however, is purely illusory, even in terms of government revenues; the individual formerly holding the government securities would have been paying taxes up to 91¼ per cent of the interest he was receiving (and would have received on the new debt had the wealth tax not been imposed). As a result of the wealth tax the government would evidently lose taxes on the wealth which it has effectively sequestered. With a 91¼ per cent tax rate the loss of tax revenues would be £73 000. (Even at an 80 per cent personal tax rate the net gain in terms of government revenues is only £16 000). It follows, therefore, that to discuss tax revenues (as does *Labour's Economic Strategy*) in terms of saving servicing costs on the National Debt is misleading unless this is amended to "Saving the net of tax cost of servicing the National Debt."

This again, however, needs to be further qualified by pointing out that savings thus realised are in any case not available for any form of welfare expenditure or reduction of taxes on income. They are only available for investment. This is simply because the wealthy taxpayer would almost certainly have been using the net of tax interest for investment. Unless the government similarly uses the £7000 for this purpose there will be a reduction in the overall level of investment and in general this is contrary to the economic interests of the nation. Indeed it is contrary to government policy, which is invariably concerned to encourage investment. In fact, if it were not to disturb the balance between private and state investment, the government would need somehow to get the £7000 back into private sector investment by allowing an extension of bank and other forms of private industry financing. Effectively therefore the net result of raising £1M taxes would be that there would be an additional extension of, say, bank lending at, say 8 per cent. The government would then obtain its normal taxes (corporation tax, dividend taxes, etc) on the unearned income flowing from this investment. But it would in any case have got its normal taxes on unearned income if in fact the £7000 had remained in the hands of the original taxpayer (the individual subject to the £1M of wealth tax) and he had invested the £7000.

Essentially, therefore, all that has happened at the end of this elaborate process is that the government is collecting tax revenues from banks and bank shareholders on the £7000 rather than from the original taxpayer, who, but for the wealth tax, would have been investing £7000. The only additional gain to the government is the net of tax income which the investor would have got from the £7000; but since this would also have been saved and invested, the government will be obliged to follow suit if it is not to reduce the level of investment in the economy.

It is possible to refine this type of analysis to cover more complex situations and to take account of other factors but these will tend to counteract one another and will not in any material sense change the above conclusion. For example, some allowance could be made for a marginal reduction in consumption by some of the less wealthy taxpayers as a result of the tax. This would give rise to a saving in real resources which could be used to provide additional benefits to lower income groups, etc. At this degree of refinement of the calculation, however, it would also be necessary to take into account the extent to which wealthy taxpayers would regard such taxation as confiscation which they forestalled directly by greater consumption of their wealth, or indirectly through gifts.

It must be concluded, therefore, that on any rational assessment, no welfare advantages in terms of resources available for giving more benefits to lower income groups would follow from greater taxation of wealth. Having regard to the possible £710M cost of wealth taxation in real resources there must in fact be a net sacrifice in the welfare of the community at large in order to pay for the economic costs of additional taxation of wealth.

Benefits: elimination of inequalities of power

The sociological arguments in favour of taxation of wealth tend to resolve themselves into two propositions. The first is that inequalities of wealth create inequalities of power because wealth gives individuals economic power over their fellows and, in a larger context, over means of communication and persuasion such as newspapers. The second is that inequalities of wealth are unfair in that they can create a privileged position for the wealthy in terms of the living standards which they can maintain, the educational and career opportunities they can obtain for their children, and so on.

Taking the inequalities of power argument first, this is inherent in any society or organisation that is not run purely and wholly on democratic lines. It is as inherent in the civil service, the armed forces, the cabinet, and in companies as it is in inequalities of wealth. The key question as regards the inequalities of power argument is quite simply whether or not the proposed method of reducing inequalities of wealth will in fact bring about greater equality of power.

It is extremely difficult to see how it can be argued that the mere transfer of legal ownership from individuals to institutions (such as the insurance companies or pension funds which might take the place of proprietors) would reduce inequalities of power. This is merely a transfer of power from individuals to institutions or, more realistically, from proprietors to the managers of the companies since institutions are rarely interested in exercising more than a limited degree of their legal authority. The inequalities of power would then continue to exist; they would be as open to abuse as formerly. Cecil King as a non-proprietorial manager of the International Publishing Corporation (IPC) could (and from time to time did) use his publications to express his own view in much the same way that Lord Beaverbrook chose to in exercising his role as a proprietorial manager.

Nor would the inequalities of power be reduced by transferring power from private individuals to the state by effective nationalisation of companies. Parliament has not the capability (nor is it conceivable that any organisation could have the capability) to control democratically hundreds of thousands of individual enterprises. There would simply be a transfer of power from proprietorial management to non-proprietorial management, with the added disadvantage that the latter could not be deposed by an internal revolution of fellow directors, shareholders or takeover bidders.

Essentially inequalities of power arise from situations of control of the commitment of resources and are a result of the demand for higher levels of material welfare which require a society organised in such a way that power must be concentrated in the hands of specialist organisations and particular individuals. Insofar as these inequalities are objectionable it is evident that they will not be overcome by replacing one source of inequality by another.

Benefits: elimination of inequalities of wealth

The social values argument against inequalities of wealth is essentially that such inequalities enable favoured individuals to achieve higher living standards, better education, etc, than the rest of the community. This is undoubtedly true.

It should be noted, however, that this is equally an argument against all inequalities of income whether brought about by inequalities of wealth or inequalities of ability. It is clearly the case that an outstanding scientist, cabinet minister, barrister or company director can achieve to all intents and purposes most of the worth-while inequalities of living standards, educational opportunities, etc, that are brought about by wealth. In other words £10 000 a year of earned income resulting from exceptional abilities will provide most of the basic inequalities which, under this argument, are regarded as objectionable.

The total number of UK taxpayers with incomes in excess of £10 000 a year in the year 1967–8 was 42 300 (Inland Revenue Statistics 1970). Of these 51 per cent, or some 21 400, were in receipt of *earned* incomes of £8000 or more. The typical unearned income of this might be around, say, £1000, representing assets of some £20 000. This level of wealth would typically be below the exemption limit of any practicable wealth tax and therefore this income group, accounting for over half of all those with more than £10 000 of income, would be unaffected by taxation of wealth. Given this, it follows that 51 per cent of the inequalities of consumption arise from earned income or such a level of unearned income as would not be affected by wealth taxes.

But the remaining 49 per cent of taxpayers with incomes in excess of £10 000 (some 20 900 taxpayers in all) only a fraction are likely to be affected by any conceivable taxation of wealth to the extent of their living standards being significantly altered.

It must therefore be concluded that even the most severe taxation of wealth would not materially alter inequalities of consumption insofar as these are regarded as arising from incomes of £10 000 or more a year.

Conclusions

The costs which would result from the elimination of the private company by higher taxation of wealth and the assumption of its functions by public companies were estimated at around £710M in higher costs, export of capital and administration. In terms of tax revenues available for consumption in the form of lower taxes on income, higher old-age pensions, etc, the yield from the imposition of more or higher taxes would be negligible, since they would be taxes on savings and wealth. No gains would arise in terms of a reduction in the inequalities of power, insofar as these inequalities arise from the control of assets since the effect of these fiscal changes would merely be the transfer of such control to managers, institutions, etc. In terms of inequalities of consumption the heavier taxation would have little material affect since the bulk of such inequalities is financed by earned income which would not be affected by such taxation.

Chapter Seven
A New Tax Policy for a Mixed Economy

The desirability of a mixed economy with a large private sector is generally accepted by all the major political parties in the UK. It would also appear to be accepted by the main parties that the overriding consideration of government policy and legislation should be the efficient operation of this mixed economy. At this point, however, the serious consideration of the principles (and even more *agreement* on the principles themselves) which should inform public policy terminates.

In the absence, however, of such guiding principles based on a comparative assessment of the contribution which each sector can make to the efficiency of the economy, the general concensus is negated or rendered ineffectual by policies and measures introduced by successive governments in an *ad hoc* manner in their attempt to resolve major long-term economic problems. This contradiction is seen very clearly in the private company sector: on the one hand, effective control and management of companies is assailed by capital gains taxes, increasingly tight estate duty legislation and the threat of a wealth tax; on the other hand, it is being assisted by investment grants, export guarantees, etc.

The principles which should form the basis of policy towards the mixed economy would require major empirical research and a volume to themselves. In the specific context of the role of the private company and business, which we have seen to account for 31 per cent of civil employment, the following comments can be made. As was seen from Chapter 4, this sector has the following highly important functions:

1 Maintaining, by its diversity and capacity for renewal, competition right across industry

2 Providing a specialised vehicle for innovation and growth which it is extremely difficult to organise and control in a quoted company, given that this commonly involves unfettered personal dedication and major long-term risks

3 Supplying the myriad and diverse markets in which production and marketing economies do not outweigh the administrative and motivational costs of size. These markets are extensive, and their efficiency must be an important contributory factor to the efficiency of the quoted sector as well as to general living standards

4 Perhaps the most important of all, in terms of quality of life, the private company must be seen as an area of opportunity for the successive generations of gifted and possibly less orthodox individuals who prefer their own companies and believe themselves to be possessed of particular talents, ideas or innovations which could best be exploited by owning their own company

These functions appear to be of major importance to the efficiency of the economy and by their nature they could not be performed with equal efficiency by larger public companies, whose fragmented shareholding results in the loss of that individual control and power of commitment which accompanies the owner manager system characteristic of private companies. A guiding principle of policy as regards this part of the mixed economy should therefore be the preservation and improvement of this sector's efficiency in respect of these functions.

Tax policy for limited reform

As will be indicated subsequently, there is a need for a radical policy of reform of the taxation of wealth in the UK. Given, however, the emotiveness of this issue and the many other demands on the political capital of governments faced with intractible economic problems, the first requirement must be for an ameliorative programme of reform. A relatively simple reform—and one which will be considered again in the wider context below—would be reform of company law to enable companies to purchase their own shares. This is already permitted in the United States and companies frequently avail themselves of this provision to purchase shares for employees, future acquisitions and to disinvest.

The advantages of this reform would be that it would enable controlling shareholders with tax liabilities in respect of their shares, to persuade the companies in which they have the controlling interest to repurchase the shares which are the subject of the tax liability. This would provide capital for meeting the tax liability and overcome the difficulty that the shares were highly unmarketable to third parties—a situation which, as suggested, would normally be the case with all but a small percentage of private companies. In addition, this measure would have the advantage that it would help preserve existing control of the company, since the shares would not be transferred to third parties but be cancelled simply by the company effectively withdrawing them. A consequential requirement of this proposal, if it is to be effective, would be assurance that the shares so purchased would not be considered as distributions for tax purposes (as is the case in the United States which has equally rigorous provisions for tax avoidance). There would, in fact, be no rational justification for an adverse tax treatment since sale of the shares to third parties for precisely the same amount of money would not have been treated as a distribution but as a normal disposal of a capital asset. A similarly related consequential requirement of this reform would be that companies would be permitted to claim that the purchase of shares in this way, in order to provide cash to meet tax liabilities of shareholders on these shares, was a justifiable reason for retaining earnings and not being subject to short-fall provisions as might be the claim of the Revenue in the context of close company legislation.

The second major element of a programme of ameliorative reform would be the abolition of the concept of deemed disposals for capital gains tax purposes. When shares (or any assets) are not in fact realised for cash but are simply transferred from one individual to another this is in effect only a transfer of savings. Given that then no consumption of the wealth is involved, the deemed disposal provision can have no practical justification to warrant its considerable burden on tax payers, particularly since the burden is heaviest on progressive companies whose shares show high capital gains.

Tax reform for the mixed economy

As experience of the last few years has shown, it is a matter of extreme complexity and difficulty to improve the performance of the economy of a developed country. In contrast, it is a matter of the utmost ease to impair its efficiency—this merely requires the enactment of measures, the costs of which exceed benefits. UK fiscal legislation—and particularly as regards taxation of wealth—has simply been directed towards the supposed ethical and political objectives; it has not been conceived as a means of bringing about a net benefit to the economy. Given this and the fact that (as discussed in Chapter 6) wealth taxation cannot by its nature produce benefits in the form of a redistribution of consumable income or permit greater expenditure on social services, it is hardly surprising that taxation of wealth for the most part simply produces disadvantages.

To have any possibility of producing a net benefit (given the inherent high costs of collection and absence of consumable tax revenues) taxation of wealth must have as its guiding principle that it is *specifically concerned with bringing about such a net benefit*. This net benefit principle must in its turn be primarily concerned with *securing better management of the assets which constitute the nation's wealth*. The following important but fairly obvious points need to be taken into account. First, even the most marginal improvements in the efficiency with which assets are utilised yields extremely large benefits. The total fixed assets of UK companies alone in 1969 was £30 900M and allowing for stocks and non-corporate assets, the total is probably nearer £60 000M. An improvement in efficiency equal to only one per cent of these material assets (leaving out of account human assets) would amount to £600M. With corporation tax at 45 per cent and dividend taxes at 41¼ per cent at least two-thirds of this would be drawn into the exchequer from company taxation alone. Moreover, these tax revenues (unlike those derived from taxing wealth) would genuinely be available for higher levels of consumption by the poorer members of the community through better social services etc.

Second, it must be accepted, and in practice is accepted, by those who hold their wealth in the form of assets important to the economy, that they have a great and material responsibility for the efficient performance of those assets, given that the efficiency of the economy is to a large extent dependent on precisely this. Hence there is the reasonable likelihood that these individuals would accept a system of taxation which had as its object, and demonstrably produced, a net benefit to the community by inducing better management of the nation's assets.

Third, the present methods of taxing wealth while complex, multifarious and crushing in their intent are nevertheless not in any way designed to bring about any improvement in the efficiency with which wealth so taxed is employed. Capital gains tax in fact levies a special tax on efficiency in the form of additional or newly created wealth. For example, an individual inheriting £*x* which he in no way improves would incur no capital gains tax. In contrast an individual building up an estate of £*x* from a negligible asset base in the form of inheritance or savings would suffer capital gains tax of 30 per cent on the whole of £*x*. Moreover, with the present law regarding gifts as deemed disposals for capital gains tax purposes, the latter tax is unavoidable while estate duty is not. The tax system has in fact become substantially biased against improvements in the efficiency with which assets are utilised compared with a simply passive ownership that involves no such improvement.

In this context the practical requirements of a tax system that might be expected to yield a worth-while net benefit are as follows:

1 A system should be simple and thus minimise collection costs, which in the case of wealth taxation tend to be extremely high
2 A rate of tax should not be so high as to have significant adverse side effects through the export or consumption of capital
3 Within the limits of 1 and 2, a system should be strongly biased in favour of efficiency in the management of assets and the creation of new wealth

A radical programme of reform which would seem to have a reasonable chance of meeting these requirements would be the following:—

1 The replacement of estate duties by a *gifts tax* at a uniform rate of 20 per cent against which would be allowed as a credit capital gains tax liability in respect of the assets in question
2 Making the first £0.25M of accumulated gifts exempt from tax. Accumulated gifts would however be defined as *gifts either made or received.* For example the individual who had received no gifts could pass on £0.25M free of gifts tax liability while the individuals who had received £0.25M or more in gifts would be obliged to pay 20 per cent on any gifts which he himself made
3 Enactment of the provisions referred to earlier to enable companies to purchase their own shares and thus provide the means of meeting gifts tax liabilities

Considering first the proposed 20 per cent rate, this it is hoped would meet the criterion of being reasonable on the grounds that efficiently managed *capital assets* should increase in real terms by appreciably more than this percentage in the intervals between, say, a family business being transmitted from one generation to the next. Given then that the tax did not exceed this rate, while capital gains liability was allowed as a credit and companies could repurchase shares, it should be possible for *the better than average* company to meet a tax liability of this level without adverse side effects.

This would nevertheless be a fairly exacting tax requirement in the context of the UK economy: the earnings per share of public companies has increased historically by around 4 per cent a year. This means that, in terms of increased profits, shares have barely kept up with the rate of inflation in retail prices, which has proceeded at almost the same rate. Hence with only this average performance the gifts tax would amount to wealth tax of 20 per cent in real terms.

The reasonably generous provisions (the "initial allowance" of £0.25M) as the starting point of the tax would enable the first creator of a modest business to pass it on free of tax liability. This would be highly desirable as an incentive for individuals to undertake creation of wealth and establish new enterprises. The successors to the family, however, would, by receiving as a gift a business worth £0.25M have exhausted the "initial allowance" and be obliged, if they were to pass the business intact to their successors, to find the means by efficient operation of the company, to meet the new tax liability.

The total change in tax revenues which would result from these proposals is extremely difficult to estimate given that there are no reliable statistics on the magnitude of gifts taking place in the UK. The amount of wealth transferred before death as gifts must however be several times the total passing at death, and hence the total tax revenues would not be reduced by the tax, although, as has already been pointed out, revenues raised by taxes on wealth are largely immaterial in the context of government expenditures or redistribution of consumption, since the taxes are essentially paid out of saving. Hence the government itself must "save" the revenues raised if it is not to create inflation.

A crucial aspect of these proposals, however, is that they must be a part of a rational and accepted policy by all the main political parties so that the gifts tax was *not* seen as yet another tax that might be piled onto the already monumental tax structure. Essentially the measures would have to be seen as producing a policy framework for efficient management and creation of capital assets within the mixed economy.

In this connection it might be noted that the philosophy behind the approach proposed above is not substantially different from that of the last

Fabian pamphlet on this subject, "The Case for Capital Taxes" by Oliver Stutchbury. This proposed a form of wealth and gifts tax in substitution for estate duty, surtax and capital gains tax, and accepted the point that the existing structure of wealth taxation is both irrational and inefficient.

The above proposals should therefore provide the basis for a rational wealth policy primarily concerned with net benefit and which should have a reasonable chance of being accepted on these grounds by responsible policy makers and tax payers. At the same time it would provide a realistic framework for the continued efficient operation of a mixed economy which—as we have argued—depends critically on the efficient management and ownership of wealth.

Appendix
"Top Ten" Private Companies by Industry

Industry-by-industry listing of UK-owned Private Companies in 1967 with total assets in excess of £50 000 (see page 20)

	NAME OF COMPANY	TOTAL ASSETS £M
FOOD	Trebor Sharps	11.6
	Weetabix	5.5
	Cranfield Bros	5.3
	Barkers and Lee Smith	3.3
	Tunnell Refineries	2.8
	Warburtons	2.3
	Carr's Milling Industries	2.2
	John A Hunter & Co	2.1
	Hull Fish Meal & Oil Co	2.0
	Richmond Sausage	2.0
DRINK	Edrington Holdings	12.0
	H P Bulmer	11.0
	Hall & Woodhouse	3.1
	J W Nicholson & Co (Holdings)	2.9
	Workington Brewery	1.7
	St Austell Brewery	1.5
	Gibbs, Mew & Co	1.5
	Wadworth & Co	1.4
	Combined Breweries (Holdings)	1.2
	Hydes Anvil Brewery	1.0
CHEMICALS	Wellcome Foundation	56.0
	British Titan Products Co	51.7

	NAME OF COMPANY	TOTAL ASSETS £M
CHEMICALS (*continued*)	Tennants Consolidated	11.1
	Lankro Chemicals	5.6
	Lancashire Tar Distillers	4.0
	Scott & Bowne	2.7
	Ward Blenkinsop & Co	2.2
	Alginate Industries	1.9
	Arthur Holden & Sons	1.8
	Hadfields (Merton)	1.4
METAL MANUFACTURE	James Neill Holdings	10.3
	Birmingham Battery & Metal Co	2.8
	Batchelor Robinson & Co	2.3
	Robert Cort & Sons	1.4
	C G Carlisle & Co	0.7
	G Perry & Sons	0.6
	Pegler & Louden	0.6
	Bonnington Castings	0.5
	Hope Works	0.5
NON-ELECTRICAL ENGINEERING	Owen Organisation	47.2
	David Brown Corporation	43.9
	Molins Organisation	18.0
	J C Bamford Excavators	11.0
	Trind Holdings	9.9
	Lansing Bagnall	8.9
	Dexion	6.0
	Fisher-Bendix	5.8
	Higgins Boughton Industries	4.9
	Rothesay Trust	3.0
	Colt Ventilation & Heating	2.7
ELECTRICAL ENGINEERING	Ferranti	37.3
	Belling & Co	6.4
	Bulpitt (Swan Brand)	5.3
	Erie Electronics	4.6
	W L Shareholding	4.3
	Bill Switchgear	1.9
	Central Equipment	1.8
	Multitone Electric Company	1.4
	Swift, Levick & Sons	1.3
	Dennis Ferranti Meters	1.2
SHIPBUILDING AND MARINE ENGINEERING	Lithgows	9.0
	Scott's Shipbuilding & Engineering Co	4.9
	Mersey Insulation Co	1.0

	NAME OF COMPANY	TOTAL ASSETS £M
SHIPBUILDING AND MARINE ENGINEERING (*continued*)	Crichton Brown	0.9
	Ailsa Shipbuilding Co	0.9
	Tyne Dock Engineering Co	0.7
OTHER METAL GOODS	Tinsley Wire Industries	7.8
	Mettoy	7.1
	Sheffield Smelting Co	5.9
	William Newman & Sons	2.6
	Aero Zip Fasteners	2.4
	John Williams of Cardiff	2.4
	Glovier Group	2.3
	C W Cheney	1.8
	W H Arnott, Young & Co	1.8
	Nuts & Bolts (Darlaston)	1.4
TEXTILES	Brintons	6.9
	John Hawkins & Sons (Holdings)	6.1
	Sir James Hill & Sons	5.9
	Readson	4.0
	Scottish Worsteds & Woollens	3.2
	Wigglesworth & Co	2.9
	Whitehead (W & J) Laisterdyke	2.8
	Robert Jowitt & Sons	1.9
	Don Brothers, Buist & Co	1.5
	John Spencer (Burnley)	1.3
LEATHER AND FUR GOODS	Booth & Co	2.0
	Leather Agencies	0.5
CLOTHING AND FOOTWEAR	C & J Clark	21.7
	British Bata Shoe Company	10.4
	Pagan	1.7
	Lambert Howarth	1.5
	Albert Martin Holdings	1.5
	John Tyler & Sons	1.3
	Howard Wall	1.1
	Millers (Gt Yarmouth)	0.9
BRICKS, POTTERY AND GLASS	Pilkington Bros	126.3
	Johnson Bros (Hanley) Ltd	13.8
	James Clark & Eaton	3.3
	Bristol & Provincial Property Investment Corp	2.8
	Bradford Glass	0.9
	Langley London	0.7

	NAME OF COMPANY	TOTAL ASSETS £M
BRICKS, POTTERY AND GLASS (*continued*)	Dennis Ruabon	0.6
	Appleby Slag Co	0.6
	P B Sillimanite Co	0.4
TIMBER	W C Ware & Sons	1.6
	Stag Cabinet	1.3
	J T Sydenham & Co	1.3
	Duncan Tucker	0.8
	Jas B Fraser & Co	0.7
	Edward Doherty	0.5
	Carrington Manufacturing Co	0.5
	Easiclene Domestic Equipment	0.5
PAPER, PRINTING AND PUBLISHING	Daily Telegraph	9.1
	MacMillan (Holdings)	6.7
	TPT	5.5
	Matthew Hodder	4.0
	James R Crompton & Bros	3.1
	Coventry Newspapers	2.9
	William Nash	2.9
	Southern Newspapers	2.9
	Broad Jesse & Co	2.1
	Link House Publications	2.0
OTHER MANUFACTURING	Robinson & Sons	7.7
	James Walker & Co	5.8
	Silent Channel & Co	2.1
	L. G. Harris & Co	1.2
	Vacu-Lug Traction Tyres	1.1
	F R Green (Holdings)	1.0
	Venus Packaging	0.8
	Rubber Latex	0.7
	Superflexit	0.7
	Saul D Harrison & Sons	0.6
CONSTRUCTION	S Pearson & Sons	87.6
	Sir Robert McAlpine & Sons	34.5
	Charles Brand & Son	22.4
	Balfour Beatty	9.4
	G J Lovell (Holdings)	8.6
	Humphreys & Glasgow	7.3
	Rush & Tomkins	6.8
	Alfred Booth & Co	6.4
	Minter Investment Co	6.2

"Top Ten" Private Companies by Industry

	NAME OF COMPANY	TOTAL ASSETS £M
TRANSPORT	Air Holdings	23.0
	BOECC Holdings	9.6
	Western SMT	5.8
	Caledonian Airway (President)	5.7
	Crosville Motor Services	4.5
	Cambrian Airways	2.7
	BKS Air Transport	2.7
	United Counties Omnibus	2.6
	London Coastal Coaches	1.4
	E A Gibson & Co	1.3
WHOLESALE DISTRIBUTION	Louis Dreyfus & Co	33.3
	Associated Octel	22.0
	Geest Industries	20.5
	C Czarnikow	9.6
	Gonzalez Byass	8.8
	Thomas Borthwick & Sons	6.7
	Agricultural Holdings Co	5.6
	Paterson Ewart Group	5.1
	Abco Petroleum Holdings	5.0
	Consolidated Scientific Instruments	3.9
RETAIL DISTRIBUTION	Littlewoods Mail Order	65.9
	J Sainsbury	42.0
	Robins & Day	6.2
	David Greig	5.3
	Fenwick	4.3
	William Thynne (Holdings)	4.0
	Blue Star Properties	2.8
	Ryecroft (Bradford) Holdings	2.5
	E. Sherry	2.3
	Etam	2.2
MISCELLANEOUS SERVICES	London Press Exchange	7.3
	S H Benson	5.8
	Blue Star Garages	2.8
	Park Lane Hotel	2.5
	University Motors (Holdings)	2.4
	Anglia Television	2.3
	Charles Barker & Sons	2.2
	Earls Court Exhibition Building	2.1
	Reeves	1.9
	Kensington Close	1.8

Index

Index